Bedside Manners

Josey Vogels

BEDSIDE MANNERS

sex etiquette made easy

HarperCollins*PublishersLtd*

Published by HarperCollins Publishers Ltd

First Edition

HarperCollins books may be purchased for educational, business, or sales promotional use through our Special Markets Department.

HarperCollins Publishers Ltd
2 Bloor Street East, 20th Floor
Toronto, Ontario, Canada
M4W 1A8

www.harpercollins.ca

National Library of Canada Cataloguing in Publication

Vogels, Josey
Bedside manners : sex etiquette made easy / Josey Vogels. – 1st ed.

ISBN 0-00-200677-4

1. Sex instruction. 2. Sex customs.
3. Sexual ethics. I. Title.

HQ31.V63 2004 646.7'7 C2004-900333-X

RRD 9 8 7 6 5 4 3 2 1

Printed and bound in the United States
Set in Rockwell
Illustrations by Ash Carter

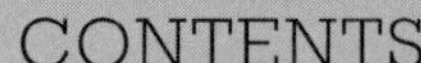

CONTENTS

Introduction

Chapter One: Let's Get Physical

Great Sexpectations **7**

Right in the Kisser **13**

The Naked Truth **14**

Chapter Two: The Other F Words: Foreplay, Fondling and Fellatio

The Warm-up **25**

Handling Yourself Properly **27**

Fellatio Finesse **29**

Chapter Three: The Main Event
First-Sex Etiquette 37
I Like It Like That 38
Are We There Yet? 40
Sound Advice 42
Coming Clean 46
Post-coital Protocol 47

Chapter Four: Awkward Moments
The Penile Code 51
Crimes of Passion 57
The Numbers Game 59
You're Only Human 61

Chapter Five: Flings and Things
One-night Wonders 67
Fling Flare 75
Booty-call Basics 77
Rebounding Rules 79
Ex Sex 80
My Best Friend's Guy 81
You've Got Mail 83

Chapter Six: Reality Check
The P's and Q's of STIs 91
A Pregnant Pause 98

Chapter Seven: The Endurance Test
Finding the Same Frequency 103
Initiation Rites 104
Passionately Speaking 106
Sextracurricular Activities 108

Chapter Eight: Mixing It Up
Wash Your Mouth Out! 119
Baring It All 122
Table Manners 124
Location Scouting 125
Pornography Protocol 126
Tantric Tips 128

Chapter Nine: Think Kink
Fantasy Forward 133
Disciplinary Action 136
Fit to Be Tied 141
Toy Story 143
The Bottom Line 148
Siderodromophilia and Other Sexual Practices They Didn't Teach You in School 151

Chapter Ten: The More the Merrier
Three's a Crowd? 155
Group Behaviour 158
In the Swing 160
Polyamory Propriety 163

Chapter Eleven: Queeries
Gaydar Love 169
Playing for Both Teams 175
Bar Code 177
Mature Choices 179

Conclusion 180

Bibliography 182

Acknowledgements 184

INTRODUCTION

Please Allow Me to Introduce Myself

I've been writing about sex for more than a decade, and in that time I've seen sex come out of the closet in a big way. Yet I'm constantly amazed at the discourteous behaviour people exhibit when getting naked with another human being. What's wrong with thanking the person with whom you just had a one-night stand, even if you'll never see him again? And it only seems polite to ask a person at an orgy if they want to have sex, rather than assume it.

I think it's safe to say that putting your hand down your pants in public and then smelling your fingers is bad etiquette, even if you are only in high school (as was the person who witnessed this event and wrote to me about it). But in other sexual situations the proper etiquette isn't always so clear. Most sex-education programs don't include sexual etiquette as part of the curriculum. And Miss Manners never explained the protocol for disposing of the used condom. Nor did she tell us what to do when someone lets one rip during the act.

Just because we're more sexually liberated doesn't mean we have to be unabashed vulgarians. Displaying good manners is a way of showing mutual respect, and respect is the cornerstone of good sex. (Yes, even when humiliating someone is part of the sex: even kinky sex requires good manners.) Unlike old-fashioned etiquette, which often consisted of sad, retrograde rules to keep women in line, modern sexual manners are about giving and getting the respect we all deserve.

You'd be amazed how far a little directness (delivered with the perfect amount of tact and charm, of course) can go towards getting what we want in bed. We all know by now—thanks to the glut of books, movies and TV shows on the subject—what it takes to meet the man of our dreams (okay, we may not have found him yet, but we know what it takes). But no one tells us what to say when the man of our dreams gets naked in front of us for the first time and we discover he has a small penis. No more counting the ceiling tiles, wondering if he's ever going to get the hint and realize it's just not happening for you. Armed with the right thing to say, or the proper way to handle a delicate situation, you'll not only feel sexually empowered, you'll be sexually satisfied. But remember that etiquette can't save you in every sticky situation, as I've learned from those who have shared their most embarrassing sex stories with me over the years. I've included some of my favourites—I call them Bedtime Stories—throughout the book. While they are intended to entertain, they also serve as a reminder that sex can be painfully awkward sometimes, and it's important to maintain a sense of humour.

When I started writing "My Messy Bedroom"—a weekly sex and relationships column—in 1994, it was an exciting time for women and sex. As late-eighties feminism was telling women that sex was something at best to be wary of, and at worst to be used against us, my girlfriends and I were sitting around drinking wine and using bananas to demonstrate our best fellatio techniques. We shared stories about our first times, our first orgasms (more often than not separate events), our favourite vibrators. It was a modern version of an age-old tradition among women. Our mothers shared recipes; we shared blowjob tips. In the same way, this book brings etiquette into the twenty-first century, and into a place where a lot of us still need a few lessons in good behaviour: the bedroom.

Now, go ahead and enjoy. No, I insist . . . after you.

Sex appeal is fifty percent what you've got
and fifty percent what people think you've got.

—**Sophia Loren,**
actress

Chapter One

LET'S GET PHYSICAL

Great Sexpectations

It would be absurd to think that one could sit down at a piano for the first time and immediately begin playing Mozart's Piano Concerto No. 24 in C Minor. Toddlers have to learn how to crawl before they can walk. You can't tackle *Ulysses* without having conquered the "I Can Read" series. (And, even still, I remain in awe of those who can finish it.) Simply put, we aren't expected to master a skill without some serious practice.

Except, it seems, when it comes to sex. Because sex is a biological urge, it's assumed that we will just "figure it all out." Of course, the mechanics of the transaction can be muddled through instinctively (insert A into B—not too difficult). But, beyond the rudimentary skills, there is an entire lifetime of sexual lessons to be learned, techniques to be sharpened, mistakes to be made and tricky situations to be navigated.

Whether it's a one-night stand or the beginnings of a beautiful relationship, getting physical with a new partner can be a challenge. From the moment you start undressing him with your eyes, you need to think about how your sexual behaviour will affect your mental and physical well-being while also being conscious of your partner's feelings. With these emotional variables to consider, plus general performance-anxiety issues, new sexual experiences can sometimes feel about as natural as Melanie Griffith's lips.

Luckily, *Bedside Manners* is here to guide you through.

Up first . . .

The waiting game

To wait or not to wait? That is the question you inevitably have to confront when you're dating someone new. You're hot for the guy but in the back of your mind is that faint but horrifying fear of being slotted into the fun-to-sleep-with-but-wouldn't-want-to-bring-her-home-to-mom category. Yes, this ridiculous, misogynistic, Madonna/whore double standard is sorely outdated, but it still lingers nevertheless. Then there's that fact that sleeping with someone takes things up a notch emotionally, and suddenly you find yourself "involved," well before you're ready.

Sure, we women are finally letting ourselves enjoy sex

without having it immediately mean "relationship," but even the most liberated among us can't always be as cavalier about it as we might like to be. If you rush into sex, no matter how hard you try to separate the physical from the emotional, those pesky feelings sneak in, rational thinking goes out the window and, next thing you know, you're convincing yourself of all kinds of things you have no business convincing yourself of this early in the game.

All this makes the age-old question of when to hop in the sack with someone new a toughie. Ultimately, more important than when to go for it is *why* you're going for it. Whether you decide to hold off or get hot, the key is to be clear about what's behind your decision. In other words, know thyself.

It's the only way to manage sexpectations.

Reasons not to have sex right away

- You're lonely.
- You don't want to hurt his feelings by saying no (otherwise known as the "mercy fuck"—not pretty).
- You think it will make him fall in love with you.
- You want to make someone else jealous.
- You're trying to get him to leave his partner.
- You're bored. (Okay, you can have sex because you're bored, but only if the other person isn't expecting anything out of it. It still kinda sucks as a reason to have sex, though.)
- He is pressuring you when you don't want to.

Quickie

A *Cosmopolitan* magazine online poll asked women how long they usually wait to have sex with a new partner. Here are the results:

The first date: **8.8%**
The second or third date: **21.4%**
After a few weeks: **33.2%**
After a few months: **36.6%**

Reasons to get busy quick

- You're horny, and he's hot.
- Sex doesn't always have to be so precious.
- You want to loosen your inhibitions.
- It's thrilling, and you only live once.
- You have nothing in common, but the physical chemistry is scorching.
- It's been a while, and you want to make sure the equipment's still working.

Dwelling issues

Admit it, the first time you walk into a guy's place, you're scanning for clues to his personality. For example, how much of a turnoff is it to find pubic hairs all over his bathroom? Or supermodel posters all over his bedroom? Thought so. Here are a few things to consider when you're having him over to your place for the first time:

- He doesn't want to see your dirty underwear all over the floor (unless that's his kink, of course, but this might be a little soon for that much information). Most guys don't like slobs either.
- I know you like to fall asleep fantasizing about (insert Current Celebrity Heartthrob here), but no guy wants to do it with a great big poster of George Clooney staring back at him. Besides, it's time to get over any lingering *Teen Beat* behaviour.
- Put away any how-to books whose titles contain the

words "Marry," "Keep" or "Make a Drooling, Doting Idiot out of," followed by the words "a Guy."

- And, yes, Rover is darned cute, but he doesn't need to watch.

Like a virgin

It's your first time out. How do you break the news to your lover? You could just "forget" to mention it—but then you miss out on some well-deserved support from your partner. You also risk him running off to tell his friends you were a mediocre lover (admit it, who's fabulous the first time out?), which is worse than simply being an inexperienced lover. Or you could simply be honest and say, "This might sound crazy, but I've never had sex. Up until now, it just hasn't felt right with anyone, but I feel ready to try it with you." Extra points for flattery, and you've probably just bought yourself a ticket to some sensitive first-time sex. Which is better than most of us can brag about. My first time was in a stack of hay in the barn. Try having a good time with hay riding up your butt!

Dry spell dilemma

Okay, so you haven't had sex in a couple of weeks—okay, months—okay, okay, you haven't been laid in two years! You simply have discriminating taste, right? Besides, you were an emotional train wreck after that last relationship, and the very idea of letting someone get too close scares the bejesus out of you. So how do you tell the total hottie you've oh-so-very-

Quickie

During Victorian times, it was not considered proper for ladies to use words that pertained to the body and its functions to describe objects. Referring to piano "legs" was considered unladylike, for example; they were to be referred to as piano "limbs." It was even decreed that piano legs must be covered to prevent offence. (Source: Harriett Gilbert and Christine Roche, *A Women's History of Sex*) slowly been letting into your life that you haven't done the nasty in two years without sounding like a charity case? Well, you have two choices: don't tell him—it's none of his business—and just hope nothing's too rusty down there (nothing a little lube won't help with, anyway); or come clean. Tell him you'd like to take things real slow because you haven't been with anyone for some time (never mind what constitutes "some" time). If he's a well-mannered lad, he'll feel flattered you deemed him dry-spell-breaking material.

Past Protocol

"The more mature girl knows that she doesn't need to resort to either slapping or running in order to deal with the too amorous boyfriend. She wards off unwelcome behavior with a firm refusal to cooperate, accompanied by a knowing smile and a suggestion of some alternative activity. She may say, 'Not now, Ambrose—let's go get a hamburger; I'm hungry.'"
(Source: Evelyn Millis Duvall, *Facts of Life and Love for Teenagers*, 1954)

Bedtime Story

"My girlfriend was rubbing back and forth on top of me, and suddenly I felt something warm in my crotch. To my horror, I looked down and saw blood coating both our torsos. At first, I thought my girlfriend had her period, but then I realized it was coming from *me*. In the heat of the moment, my Johnson had slipped out of my pants and was brutally sliced by my girlfriend's razor-like zipper. I used an entire box of Kleenex to stop the bleeding, sat on the edge of consciousness for about an hour, and now I have a scar that makes my penis look like a smiling Cyclops from certain angles." **(Michael, 28)**

Right in the Kisser

The first time you kiss someone can be electric and intensely intimate. It can also make or break an encounter if you don't handle it correctly.

Do

- Move beyond the mouth and use your lips to lightly brush an eyebrow or a cheekbone.
- Find your partner's magic spots.
- Put sex out of your mind and focus just on kissing.
- Tease. Till it hurts.
- Vary technique and speed.
- Breathe.
- Try to avoid excessive and embarrassing sound effects.
- Practise good dental hygiene.

Don't

- Engage in random, insensitive tongue-plunging.
- Abandon kissing once you head south.
- Slobber.
- Belch.
- Check your watch.
- Be a lip masher.
- Be limp-lipped.
- Suck on your partner's tongue too hard (most of us are fond of our taste buds).
- Give hickeys. We're only trying to simulate those great necking sessions in high school, not relive them.

Quickie

In the Taoist sexual tradition of China, great emphasis was placed on sensual kissing, which was considered so erotic and private that even to this day the Chinese rarely kiss in public. (Source: Sarah Dening, *The Mythology of Sex*)

The Naked Truth

The unveiling

No matter how you get naked in front of each other for the first time—tearing each other's clothes off in a fit of passion on your way to the bedroom or shyly disrobing in the dark and then diving under the covers with the lights off—there are certain things you should never do on first glimpse of him in all his glory. Pointing at his crotch and laughing, for example, is clearly a no-no.

And, ladies, pulling the sheets up to your neck and flinching when his hands come anywhere near your tummy is hardly a polite way to introduce him to your nakedness. As much as you think he's focusing on your flaws, most guys are simply thrilled to have a real live naked woman in front of them. And once you've come this far, it does seem a bit rude to get all self-conscious. Take a lesson from something one sweet young fella once told me: "It's not that guys aren't self-conscious about their bodies, but it's not exactly what we're focusing on the first time we're naked with you." In other words, stop worrying about what you look like and enjoy the scenery. This is one time when it is appropriate to stare—at least a little.

The first time you get naked with him . . .

Do

- Freely compliment his best features.
- Strut your stuff. A less-than-perfect but confident body is way sexier than a self-conscious perfect body.

- Unwrap yourself slowly to drive him crazy.
- Better yet, get him to unwrap you as slowly as he can possibly stand.
- Keep something on to leave a little to the imagination (socks don't count).

Don't

- Point and laugh.
- Tell him you don't mind small penises, really.
- Ask him if he's ever thought of working out.
- Tell him you think pot-bellies are sexy (yes, it's great if you really do, but save this for when you're more comfortable together).
- Act ashamed of your own body and hide yourself under the covers so he can't see it.
- Show him how you can make funny faces with your tummy rolls.

In the dark

You want to do it in the dark. He wants the lights on. Who caves? You probably want to do it in the dark because you're premenstrual, feeling bloated, haven't been to the gym in weeks and think that as long as he can't see the three-inch stubble on your legs, he won't know it's there. Oh, and you're wearing granny panties. All perfectly legitimate reasons to keep him in the dark, but let's look at the situation from his point of view.

He wants the lights on because he's been looking at porn ever since he could get it up and gets off on visuals. You

What the Canuck!

July 1991: On a hot, humid day in Guelph, Ontario, Gwen Jacob strolls down the street topless, asserting she has just as much right to go topless as men. The court eventually agrees, and it becomes legal for women to go topless in Ontario.

What the Canuck!

People in Alberta and British Columbia are more likely to sleep nude than people in any other province. (Source: A 1999 survey on Canadian attitudes about nudity compiled for the Federation of Canadian Naturists by Market Facts)

may find it hard to believe, but he wants to see your naked butt!

This is why God invented candles (I actually have no idea who invented candles, but let's go with God 'cause it's fun to use His name in a sex book). Candles are the perfect lights on/lights off compromise. They make everyone look sexy. And, if you're feeling adventurous, you can always get kinky and drip wax on each other. Just be sure to avoid coloured wax and beeswax, as these get too hot. Use paraffin and drop it from a height so it has a little time to cool down before hitting each other's bits. (See Chapter Nine for advice on how to introduce kinky play.)

In a flap?

He drops his drawers, and you look down and see he's "Canadian" (inexplicably, this has become a pet name for an uncircumcised penis). Growing up in North America, where well over half of the male population is circumcised, you've perhaps never encountered an uncut penis. So what do you do when you're suddenly staring into the eye of a penis *au natural*?

Do

- Take advantage of its built-in lubricating action.
- Ask how he likes his stick handled (I know it sounds crazy, but you're allowed). He may like the skin pulled back for oral and not for manual stimulation, or vice versa.
- Pull the foreskin back when putting on a condom. If you

don't, the condom can get trapped inside the foreskin, reducing sensitivity and effectiveness, never mind making him feel like he has a plastic bag wedged inside his willy.

Don't

- Wince, blanch or scream.
- Say, "Eeewww, what's all that extra skin doing there?"
- Squish it into funny shapes like the "baby bird" and the "Eskimo smile" (use your imagination). It might break the ice, but it probably won't get anybody very hot.
- Think that because he's uncut he's naturally less clean. If he can wash his car until it gleams, surely he can keep a few little folds of skin clean. I mean, gals manage to clean all their foldy bits, and we can't even pull it out in the shower for better access.
- Yank down his turtleneck and start patting him on the head. The poor guy's not used to being exposed and is extra sensitive.

Sizing things up

Oddly enough, guys don't seem to mind if you say, "Holy shit, be careful or you'll put an eye out with that thing." It's trickier to know what to say if, well, you know you'll be giving your girlfriends the old pinky signal in the morning. If you want to have sex that night, it's best not to say anything at all and hope that what he lacks in size he's learned to make up for in other departments. After all, we're the ones always assuring guys that size doesn't matter. Okay, it matters a bit, but, honestly,

Quickie

Over 80% of the world's males are uncircumcised. The U.S. is the only country in the world that routinely circumcises most of its male infants for non-religious reasons. Routine infant circumcision started in the U.S. in the 1870s, when it was promoted as a preventative cure for masturbation. (Sources: E. Wallerstein, "Circumcision"; John Harvey Kellogg, *Plain Facts for Old and Young*) given the choice between a guy with a huge schlong and a guy with a skilful tongue and hands, wouldn't you choose door number two? After all, vaginas are pretty stretchy things, sort of a one-size-fits-all deal. Which is not to say we don't like a little meat in his muscle. But I've always considered penises to be like snowflakes: no two are alike, and they all have their own personal charm. Be kind and show it a little appreciation:

- Find something endearing about his dick and focus on that. "You have such a smooth/warm/inviting/lovely penis/cock/dick."
- Don't ever tell a guy he's got a cute *little* penis.
- Unless you've been together for a while (and even then I find the practice questionable), don't give his pecker a private pet name.
- Don't overcompensate. You'll only distort his ego and make it harder on him if his next girlfriend decides to be brutally honest.
- Try not to sound like a bad porn movie when talking about his penis, but do indulge him in some cheesy porn dialogue once in a while. Hey, you make him go see chick flicks sometimes, right?
- Of course, just like your momma told you, if you can't say anything nice, don't say anything at all.

Piercing parlance

It'd be rude to point and say "What the hell is that?" when he drops his drawers and you discover he's adorned. Much more polite would be to say, "My, what a beautiful ampallang you have." To that end, here's a guide to genital piercings:

For him

Ampallang—Passes horizontally through the body of the glans or penis head, whether through the urethra or above it.
Apadravya—A vertical piercing through the glans that usually traverses the urethra.
Dydoe—Passes through the top ridged edge of the penile glans.
Foreskin—A piercing through the foreskin.
Frenum—A piercing through the surface skin on the shaft of the penis just below the head (not entering the urethra or the shaft core).
Guiche—A piercing through the skin between the anus and scrotum; weights are often worn for additional stimulation.
Hafada—A piercing on the upper sides of the scrotum.
Prince Albert—A piercing that enters the top of the penis glans and exits at the bottom of the penis head. (The reverse PA exits the top of the glans.)
Scrotal—A piercing through the skin of the scrotum. See also Hafada.

For her

Clitoris—A piercing directly through the clitoris.
Hood—A horizontal or vertical piercing that passes through

the clitoral hood. Ideally, the bead of the ring rests on the aroused clitoris.

Inner labia—Passes through the labia minora (inner lips); paired labia piercings may be "locked" with a single piece of jewellery as a chastity or infibulation device.

Outer labia—A piercing that passes through the labia majora (outer lips).

Triangle—Passes underneath the clitoral shaft.

His and hers

Navel—A piercing through the rim of the navel.

Nipple—A piercing through the nipple; may be vertical, horizontal or at any other desired angle.

Hair-raising hurdles

Many North Americans are offended by body hair. Personally, I've always had a bit of a soft spot for those seventies porn films where everyone is furry and proud. Then I got my first Brazilian wax job and everything changed. You have to admit, it's a lot more fun performing oral sex on someone when you don't have to stop and pick pubes out of your teeth.

Does that mean it's cool to ask a partner to trim? Some women find it a real affront, as if he's saying you aren't good enough in your natural state. And goodness knows, we get enough of this everywhere else in our lives, we could use a break from it in the comfort of our own bedrooms (or his, as the case may be). And how many guys are willing to have hot wax slathered on their crotches and then have someone rip out the hair?

If he wants you to trim, shave, wax or pluck, ask if he'd be willing to do the same. You can make it part of the fun. Tell your partner you're willing to let him shave your crotch, if he'll let you shave his. It can be funny and sexy. Just make sure you're sober. Sharp objects and booze don't mix.

You can always get creative with your pubic hair. One guy told me he slept with a woman who had three-inch-long braids in her pubes, and another gal told me she dyed her entire pubic region bright green. Hey, pubic hair can be pretty dull stuff—might as well have a little fun.

Quickie

It was considered elegant for aristocratic ladies of the 16th century to let their pubic hair grow as long as possible so it could be pomaded and adorned with bows and ribbons. (Source: Sexualtips.com)

I mean, if you were a bloke, would you pu
it in a mouth, where there are teeth? The teeth of a female who's been discriminated against for centuries?

—**Kathy Lette,
author**

Chapter Two

THE OTHER F WORDS: FOREPLAY, FONDLING AND FELLATIO

The Warm-up

In my opinion, the word "foreplay" undermines the importance of the act. It makes it sound like a rather dull and tedious way to pass time until you get to "the real thing." When, really, foreplay is as important—and delicious—as "the main event." I like to call it the warm-up or, if you prefer, the if-we-don't-spend-a-lot-of-time-getting-me-worked-into-a-frenzy-now-you're-going-to-suffer-some-wicked-tongue-lash-later-sweetie period of lovemaking. And, as with most things sexual, there is appropriate and inappropriate behaviour when it comes to this yummy stage.

Do

- Mix it up. Yes, he likes variety, too.
- Communicate. He can't read your mind.
- Solicit details. Of course it feels good, but ask him what you can do to make it feel *reeeally* good.
- Tease. I know some guys think five minutes feels like a lifetime—maybe it's from watching so many porn videos in which the participants are naked and screwing before you can say, "How do you unhook this thing?"—but prolong the anticipation . . . and then wait some more.
- Take foreplay beyond the bedroom: sexy emails, notes, a little something whispered in his ear when he leaves for work in the morning. Go gitch-free and let him know partway through the evening.
- Touch places that get neglected: the backs of knees, the inside of elbows, earlobes . . .
- Rediscover the kid in you and play (the one part of the word "foreplay" I do like).

Don't

- Answer the phone (especially if it's family calling).
- Use this time to discuss the future of the relationship. (I swear, people have told me this has happened to them.)
- Get into a rut. You know what I'm talking about: kissing, three minutes; oral sex, two minutes; and suddenly, he's in!
- Let him steal home plate when you're only on first.

- Close your mind. The best foreplay is all about using your imagination.

Handling Yourself Properly

Now that doctors are pretty sure masturbation doesn't cause insanity, vomiting, epilepsy or any of the other nasty things they believed around the turn of the last century, there's no reason not to DIY. That said, there are some things to take into consideration when waving hello to the little man in the canoe:

- *The walls have ears.* No matter how positive your roommates, neighbours or family members happen to be about the joys of masturbation, they probably don't want to hear you getting intimate with yourself. Keep screams, slaps and hoots to a minimum. And if you're using toys, try to avoid the ones that sound like industrial floor polishers.
- *Be considerate in public.* Yes, I know it's a long, boring train/plane/bus ride, but others have to use the bathroom to pee, so if you must slip in for a quick wank, keep the sessions brief and discreet. Back in your seat, a well-placed blanket in your lap may seem like a polite way to enjoy self-pleasure, but the stranger sitting next to you may think differently. I suppose you could always check with him to see if he minds, but that's seems a little inappropriate. If you simply can't resist, at least wait until he's asleep.

Quickie

In 1848 the American religious zealot Sylvester Graham—who blamed the nation's sinful excesses on too much meat and spicy food—invented the graham cracker as a nice bland dietary substitute that would reduce the nation's sex drive and save souls. (Source: Richard Zacks, *History Laid Bare*)

- *Play nice with others.* "Mind if I wank off in front of you?" isn't the most polite way to introduce masturbation with a partner. You might want to try something a little more seductive. Here are two suggestions: "Hey, sexy, I'd love to masturbate for you and show you how I make myself come" or "Hey, sexy, it'd be such a turn-on to watch you get yourself off. Would you grant me that pleasure?" That way you turn it into a favour to you as opposed to something selfish on your partner's part. Clever, no?

Masturbating in front of your partner actually does you both a big favour. It creates a level of comfort that can lead to some hot sex. And besides being a huge turn-on, watching someone else masturbate can teach you loads about what it takes for your partner to reach orgasm. As they say, a picture is worth a thousand words. But remember your manners. While masturbating, at least try to make it look like you remember that your partner is still there. Mutual masturbation is also good fun. Just make sure you're both comfy (side by side works best, I find) to avoid unnecessary kinks and strains.

Bedtime Story

"At age 11, I used to use hand cream from my mother's medicine cabinet to masturbate. I think she knew what was going on and tired of buying new lotion every four days, so she hid the stuff. I found a can of self-tanning lotion that felt just as good and used it up in just two days. While I was changing into my baseball uniform before a game, my stepdad came into my room. He said he wanted to be sure I was wearing my protective cup properly and asked that I remove it and wash the cup out. Well, when I removed the jockstrap, there it was: my self-tanned, pumpkin orange tool. He assured me he wouldn't say anything to my mom, but I'm sure he did. I've never heard two people laughing so hard in all my life." **(Alistair, 29)**

Fellatio Finesse

While I have heard a few complaints from men about women who don't seem to know what they're doing down there, guys are generally happy to have a tongue and a set of lips doing just about anything with their privates. Although men may not be fussy, there are a few proprieties that should be honoured when performing the art of fellatio:

- Move in slowly. Sudden movements may frighten the poor thing.
- You're not bobbing for apples. Think about what you like when it comes to oral sex: a little pressure, lots of slow, long licks and plenty of teasing. Get your hands, lips, tongue and mouth in on the action.
- Look like you're enjoying yourself. Make eye contact while you're down there. Give him a wink and a smile that says, "I'm havin' fun, howzabout you, baby?"

I do not give blowjobs. Why not? Because I find it really off-putting, seeing a grown man look that pathetically grateful.

—Jenny Éclair, comedian

- Don't neglect the surrounding areas: balls, bum cheeks, thighs, tummy, hips. Be careful, though—some guys are ticklish.
- Contrary to popular belief, teeth aren't always a bad thing. No need to leave marks, but a gentle scrape or a light nibble can add pressure and feel good.
- Don't lose focus. When things get intense, and he's about to come, don't choose that moment to try something new . . . unless you want to keep him on the edge for a while (also fun).
- If you're not sure he likes what you're doing, you're allowed to ask for feedback.
- Have fun. Despite its common name, it shouldn't feel like a job (oh, and you probably shouldn't blow either).

Oral exam

If you want to be orally confident, learn to talk the talk:

Autofellatio—Performing fellatio on yourself. Apparently, one in 2,000 men can do this.

Cunnilingus—Oral sex performed on a woman. From the Latin *cunnus* (vulva) and *lingere* (to lick).

Deep throat—A term made famous by a seventies porn movie of the same name, this is the practice of taking a man's penis deep into your mouth while performing fellatio.

Dental dams—A rectangular piece of latex rubber that is placed over the labia or anus during oral-vaginal or oral-anal sex.

Fellatio—Oral sex performed on a man. From the Latin *fellare*, to suck.

Rimming—Also referred to as analingus. Refers to the act of licking or inserting the tongue into your partner's anus.

69 or *soixante-neuf*—The act of performing oral sex on your partner while he does the same to you, putting your bodies into a position that looks like the number 69.

Getting a "head" of yourself

Despite the ever-increasing popular belief that a blowjob is not sex (thanks, Mr. Clinton!), placing your mouth over someone's genitals is undeniably more intimate than a peck on the cheek at the end of the night. Some would even argue that oral sex is more intimate than intercourse. If, for whatever reason, you decide to go the oral-sex-only route, you still need to consider timing. Offering to go down on him for dessert after dinner on a first date—while an exciting way to introduce it—might be moving a little too fast. Beyond that, as long as both parties agree and you say please and thank you and don't do it in mixed company, use your own discretion when deciding when to engage in some oral communication. Though again, as with intercourse with someone new, know thyself. Make sure you're doing it for the right reasons and that you're ready to deal with your feelings and expectations afterwards. Can you handle it if he decides to eat and run? I know it's rude, but it happens, and you need to be emotionally prepared.

Quickie

Empress Wu Hu, who ruled during the great T'ang Dynasty (AD 700–900) forced all government officials and visiting dignitaries to pay homage to her Imperial Royal Highness by performing cunnilingus upon her. (Source: Brenda Love, *The Encyclopedia of Unusual Sex Practices*)

Past Protocol

"A daily bath may be a desirable luxury—it is not necessarily an essential, but a daily careful bathing of the hips and thighs and sexual organs should be encouraged for both men and women." (Source: Rev. Alfred Henry Tyrer, *Sex, Marriage and Birth Control: A Guide-book to Sex Health and a Satisfactory Sex Life in Marriage* [Marriage Welfare Bureau, Toronto, 1936])

Mouth to mouth

It can be hot to kiss after, or even during, oral sex. Not all guys agree with me on this point, however. If he is screwing up his face like he's just sucked a lemon as you're about to plant a big wet one on him post-blowjob, chances are he's not so into sharing. If you're unsure, you can always give your mouth a wipe on the sheets on the way up.

Bedtime Story

"My guy and I were driving to go camping when we got talking about what we were going to do to each other sexually when we got to our campsite. I decided I couldn't wait and unzipped his fly to give him a blowjob while he was driving. He had to pull over, and as I continued to go down on him, there was a knock at the window and a bright light shining into the car. My boyfriend rolled down the window and tried to cover up his erection, while I blushed like crazy and started laughing my head off. The cop just smiled and told us to be on our way." **(Jen, 31)**

Oral hygiene

What if it smells like an old gym bag down there? Pinching your nose and saying, "Eeeew, gross! What is that stench? Don't you ever bathe, boy?" is probably not going to get you a return invite. However, gagging is already enough of an oral sex hazard—him smelling like a locker room isn't going to help matters. Naturally, people sweat, and things can get funky down there—we gals aren't always daisy-fresh either—but it's nothing a little soap and water can't fix. Tell him you want to get really wet and seductively drag him down the hall into the shower. If he gets suspicious, no need to be coy about it. Growl sexily in his ear, letting him know how much you want to go down on him and, no offence, you'd enjoy it so much more if he was squeaky clean. He'll appreciate your honesty and the fact that you're taking charge. Or he'll just go with it because he's getting a blowjob out of the deal.

Spit or swallow?

You're mid-blowjob, things are clipping along nicely, and you realize he's about to blow. You've only got a split second to make the decision—spit or swallow? You weigh the pros and cons. Swallowing is tidy. It makes him feel special. It's also kinda gross and, if you have cuts in your mouth or you've just brushed your teeth, it can be dangerous.

Given that this is a matter of personal taste, there are no hard and fast rules here. However, if you absolutely refuse to swallow, at least be discreet about it. Try not to spit it out too violently and then sprint to the bathroom to gargle. A woman I know shared a trick she uses that allows her to get away with not swallowing while still turning him on. She lets him come in her mouth and slowly lets it trickle out the side. Sexy for him, no swallowing involved for her. Smart, huh?

Not only is swallowing a matter of personal taste, it can be a

What the Canuck!

June 26, 2003: Vancouver-based actresses Tanya Seltenrich and Dana Williams perform oral sex on each other as part of a play/performance art piece billed as Canada's first live sex show. Despite threats by local authorities to shut the show down, no arrests are made. (Source: canoe.ca)

matter of physical taste, as well. You might want to pin this one up on the fridge door for your honey. Though some experts insist that diet doesn't affect the taste of a man's come, others insist that of vegetarians taste better and that foods such as pineapple, kiwi and parsley will also sweeten his load. To be avoided? Red meat, cigarettes, coffee, alcohol and asparagus.

Profile: The Abstainer

You know the old adage "It's better to give than to receive"? Well, apparently not everyone lives by those words, especially when it comes to oral sex. In what seems to me the most egregious violation of good breeding, there are people out there who actually expect to receive oral sex but refuse to return the favour. Emily Post must be turning in her grave. So listen up, all you ladies out there who refuse to "play the flute": if you won't do it for yourself, take one for the team, sister. The more selfish gals out there, the more reason guys will have to refuse us.

Some women say it makes them gag. We're not asking you to re-enact *Deep Throat*. You can do a lot with your mouth that won't trigger the gag reflex, so I'm afraid that excuse is a little lame. And no, you don't have to swallow (see "Spit or Swallow?" on page 33).

As for who does whom, and when, I'm not a fan of the old 69—it splits my focus. But moving back and forth—a little for him, a little for you—is a perfectly polite way to enjoy some oral pleasure.

An orgasm is a way of saying you enjoyed yourself, even as you compliment a host on a wonderful spinach quiche.

—Helen Gurley Brown,
author and former editor
of _Cosmopolitan_ magazine

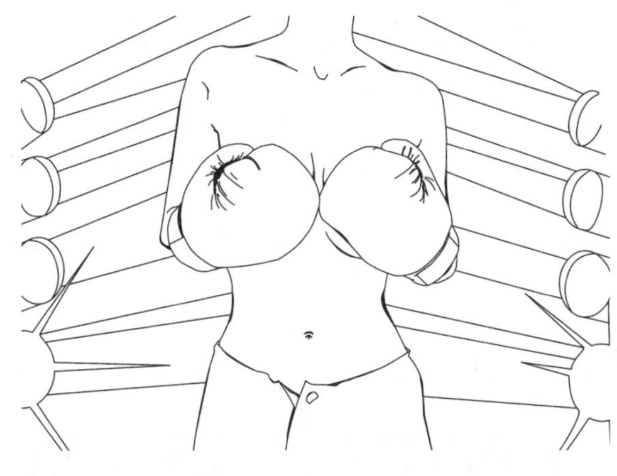

Chapter Three

THE MAIN EVENT

First-Sex Etiquette

Most of us go into our first sexual encounter completely in the dark, often quite literally. And, as I keep saying, sex usually takes a few kicks at the can to become fun. Luckily, practice makes perfect. There are, however, a few thoughtful things a couple can do to make the first time much more memorable:

- Plan ahead. While there is something to be said for spontaneity, when it comes to the first time, it's good manners to talk about it beforehand so you can set things up.

- Location, location, location. Create a comfortable, low-pressure, romantic but fun environment, and the rest should follow quite nicely.
- Keep your expectations in check. This will stop you from desperately trying to fulfill fantasies about what the encounter should be, making it easier for you to be sensitive to the reality of the situation and each other's needs.
- If he's already had sex, get him to talk with you about it and tell you what to expect. Ask him to teach you what he knows. A big turn-on for him, beneficial to you. Vice versa if it's his first time out and you've already got a notch or two on your bedpost.

I Like It Like That

We all know that good sex is about healthy communication—being able to tell your partner what works and doesn't work for you. However, there are proper ways of doing this. You don't want to lie there while he's developing a serious neck kink, knowing he's about an inch off target. On the other hand, "What are you doing, you freak?" might be a little harsh. While directness and honesty are laudable communication strategies, we all need positive encouragement to improve.

So, as much as it might be nice to order up your sexual needs as you would a large fries at a fast-food restaurant, telling someone what you do and don't like in bed is a delicate task. Egos are at stake. Approach with caution:

- The longer you've been with someone, the more directly you should be able to ask for what you want—politely, of course. Even though you'd like to smack him when he tweaks your nipple in that way you've told him a million times you hate, be nice.
- A fresh candidate deserves some leeway to figure out what you like. Some strategic hip wiggling, well-placed moans, even some hands-on guidance, are all acceptable in the early stages and beyond.
- Watch porn together. Let him know what you like and don't like.
- Go sex-toy shopping together. It's a great way to open up a discussion about sexual preferences.
- Talk about what turns you on in non-sexual situations. Long car rides are good for this. "Mmm . . . baby, I was just thinking about that time you did X. I'd love to do that again sometime, and maybe next time we could add Y."
- Bring hand puppets to bed and act out your sexual desires. (Okay, yes, I'm kidding, but actually, demonstrating how you like to be handled on the web between your thumb and forefinger can be quite instructional.)

Quickie

Sometimes it's easier to talk about what gets you off in completely non-sexual situations. It's also a great way to pass the time as you're waiting for the bus or in line at the supermarket. It's usually best to be with your partner at the time. Strangers might not be so open to the concept. Then again . . .

What the Canuck!

Stonehenge is a massive fertility symbol, according to Canadian researcher Anthony Perks, a retired professor of obstetrics and gynecology at the University of British Columbia. Perks suggests that, viewed from above, Stonehenge—built between 3,000 and 1,600 BC—resembles the anatomy of the human vulva: the inner bluestone circle represents the labia minora; the giant outer sarsen stone circle is the labia majora; the altar stone is the clitoris; and the open centre is the birth canal. (Source: Dr. Anthony Perks and Darlene Marie Bailey, "Stonehenge: A View from Medicine," *Journal of the Royal Society of Medicine*, July 2003.)

Are We There Yet?

Women have harped for years on the importance of their pleasure, and as a result many guys have fallen into the "Ladies First" approach to sex. In other words, let's get our orgasm out of the way so he can come and pass out guilt-free. It's not necessarily a bad rule, but it doesn't mean you want him going at it until you're chafing just because he's trying not to come before you do.

Sometimes, it's just not going to happen. You've counted the ceiling tiles. You've gone over tomorrow's to-do list—several times. You've reviewed the birthdays of every family member and friend that's coming up in the next six months. And yet, there he is, pumping away—looking dangerously close to cardiac arrest—and if he asks you one more time, "Well, did you?" you'll scream, and not with pleasure.

It's fine to tell him. Then things can become less goal-oriented and you can shift the focus back to simply having fun. If he comes first, so what? You can catch the next train. Of course, if he comes first and you still want your orgasm, even in his post-orgasm stupor, a gentleman will at least try to help you out, even if it just means holding you—and, yes, staying awake!—while you take care of things. Same goes if you come first. Be considerate. After basking in your post-orgasm bliss for a minute or two, give him a hand finishing up.

G-spot check

Every so often—with the right amount of arousal, stimulation and aligning of the planets—a girl may find herself squirting just like the boys. Congratulations, you've just ejaculated! G-spot orgasms result from the right amount of clitoral/urethral stimulation combined with pressure and stimulation along the inside upper wall of the vagina. Despite the recent focus on female ejaculation experiences, a gal should never feel inadequate—or be made to feel inadequate by her partner—if she hasn't had a G-spot orgasm. Some women can train themselves to ejaculate on demand, while most of us discover this sensation by accident at some point in our sexual lives. If it happens by surprise, there's no need to be grossed out. It may feel like you've peed the bed, but rest assured, it is not pee.

Given that women can ejaculate anywhere from two tablespoons to two cups of fluid (compared to a guy's measly two teaspoons of ejaculate), if you are a regular ejaculator, you might want to invest in some surgical pads or plastic sheets out of consideration to your partner (who may have to sleep in the same bed you just soaked). Taking precautions is both polite and fiscally responsible: one woman I know destroyed several futons before adopting this method.

Faking it

Is faking it poor etiquette? Well, I guess if you're a convincing actress and your partner can't tell, you're not technically being rude to him. You are, however, setting a trap for yourself. How do you tactfully go from faking it to having a real orgasm? If you suddenly discover you're the strong, silent type when you come, your partner may well wonder what happened to the screaming banshee he thought he was with.

Past Protocol

"Do not get into the habit of pretending your passion has been aroused and that you have enjoyed an orgasm, thinking thereby to please your husband." (Source: Rev. Alfred Henry Tyrer, *Sex, Marriage and Birth Control*)

Quickie
In an online survey of more than 15,000 people at Queendom.com, 70% of women and 25% of men admitted to having faked it at least once.

What if you decide to stop faking and your partner freaks and gets insecure when he realizes he can't make you come after all? You can see why it's not worth it.

So how do you politely get out of the trap? Well, I wouldn't encourage you to hop into bed tonight and say, "Hate to break it to you, big guy, but showtime's over. I want a real orgasm for once, goddammit!" Instead, try following these steps:

1. Ease up on your performances until you eventually have a few lovemaking sessions where you don't come at all.
2. Your partner will no doubt become concerned. You can then admit that, for some reason, you haven't been able to come lately—stress, death of a friend's cat, basically anything that isn't about your partner.
3. Together you can figure out how to make you orgasmic "again." Only this time it'll be the real deal.

Sound Advice

House rules
While we'd all love to sweep our various paramours back to the luxury penthouse we share with no one but our purebred Pomeranian, it's more likely that we'll have to drag him home to our walk-up, where our roommate will be flaked out on the couch eating day-old pizza and watching late-night *Bonanza* reruns.

Sure, the images you had of coming home, tearing each other's clothes off and doing it on the living-room coffee table may get thwarted when you share a place, but the sex you have when you have roommates can be furtive and fun. When you invite a lover into your lair, explain your living situation so he knows what he's in for. If your roommates are up, offer a quick hello and introductions if this is a first-time visit. Then lead loverboy to your bedroom, which is of course well appointed for just such an occasion so it can be instantly converted into a love den.

Just remember that no matter how much you love or hate the people with whom you share lodging, no one wants to hear you scream or call him "Mr. Big." Keep the groaning to a minimum. Have fun with it. As great as it is to let yourself go wild in the sack, it can be also be hot when you have to reign yourself in. There's something kind of sexy about a man biting into your pillows in ecstasy, no?

Bedtime Story

"I was home one night with my boyfriend, and my sister, who was going to bed, asked me to answer the phone if it rang as she was waiting for a call. My boyfriend and I started fooling around, and sure enough the phone rang. I answered on the cordless and went upstairs to wake my sister, who picked up the phone in her room. I went back downstairs, and my boyfriend chased me into my room. Just as I was about to put the phone on the stand, he grabbed me

> and the phone fell to the floor. I thought, 'No big deal. I hung up the phone. I can put it on the charger later.' We then proceeded to have the most amazing, loudest sex we've had in a while. Afterwards, we were lying in bed when my little sister walked in and said, 'Guys, the next time you fuck like that, make sure the damn phone is hung up.'" **(Emilie, 26)**

Noisy nookie

There is nothing quite as fabulous as having someone completely let go with you in the sack. It sure beats the hell out of having a guy so terrified of making noise that he looks like his head is about to pop off while doing it. That only makes you want to scream, *"Just let go!"*

Maybe it's because I grew up in a house full of noisy people, but I like a little racket in bed. There's nothing like a little vocal encouragement to acknowledge a job well done. It's good for the ego. It's also helpful in getting what you want. Just crank up the volume a notch when he gets something right, and he'll get the message.

Sex noises need not be elaborate, just sincere. And while it might be nice to come up with something that doesn't make you sound like a bad porn movie, "Yes, yes," "Oh God," and "I'm coming" (if you need to get more specific) will all work. Whatever lets the other person know things are pretty much all good. Insults, jokes and armpit farts are best avoided. Unless, of course, that's what you're into.

On the other hand, if you're thinking about what you're saying or what noise you're making, you're doing something wrong. The best kind of sex is when you are so wildly passionate that you don't know if you were loud or not.

Bedtime Story

"After having sex in an airplane bathroom, my girlfriend and I emerged only to be confronted by two flight attendants and loud applause from the nearby passengers. I guess we had been less tactful than we thought. As we were being escorted to our seats, red-faced, we realized that we must have been amusing our fellow passengers for several minutes, yet no one had interrupted us. The flight attendants said they were just about to put a stop to our activity when they determined that we were obviously 'wrapping it up.'"
(Dominic, 32)

Sorry, but I couldn't help overhearing . . .

While it's one thing to be a participant in a knockdown, drag 'em out, screaming sex session, it's quite another to be on the other side of the wall of one. So what do you do? A good bang on the wall might slow the loud and lusty pair down for a bit, but chances are they either won't hear you, won't care or will be back at it again just in time to jar you awake as you're about to drift off. If you're too embarrassed to confront them, you could do what a neighbour of mine once did and draw a little storyboard explaining the situation and pin it to your neighbour's door.

You could try the passive approach: the next time you see the couple, casually work a comment into the conversation like, "Have you ever noticed how thin the walls are between our places?" Toss in a cocked eyebrow and they should get the hint. Or you could do the cowardly thing and tell the superintendent or property owner and let him or her handle it. If none of this works, there's one last resort. Call the cops. Just don't ever expect to be invited to join in the fun.

What the Canuck!

In a Canadian landlord and tenant court battle in 1990, a young woman was evicted from her apartment for moaning during intercourse. A former neighbour testified that her family had moved after being awakened by the woman's enthusiasm several nights a week, as often as 2 or 3 times a night, for periods of 30 to 60 minutes. (Source: Jeffrey Miller, *Ardor in the Court!*)

Coming Clean

Dealing with the wet spot

One of the tidiest ways to avoid having to deal with the wet spot altogether? Condoms. But if you're not using them, things can get messy. Some folks like to keep a roll of toilet paper by the bed to soak things up after a nice romp. I'm not a fan of this, as TP sticks to the sheets and you end up with little bits of it all over the place. However, lying in a pool of cold spunk isn't exactly mood-enhancing, so it's perfectly acceptable to grab a towel or something quasi-clean from the hamper to sop up the mess. You can then lie on it if you're both up for some post-coital snuggling. One couple told me they use hand towels of a particular colour and pattern, which they keep in a drawer next to the bed, exclusively for this purpose. One use, and into the dirty hamper they go!

Disposable pads or absorbent sheets (try luvliners.com) also make cleanup a breeze, especially if the wet spot is the result of a juicy G-spot orgasm.

King-size beds are also handy for avoiding the wet spot—simply move to drier pastures for cuddling.

He shoots . . .

Where you let a guy come is a matter of personal taste and depends on what you're comfortable with. Some gals are happy to be showered in the stuff, while others prefer to restrict their facials to the spa. Obviously, it's not the kind of thing you ask a woman about over dinner, but he should definitely check with you before making a deposit.

If a guy does come on you, he should at least offer to clean it up. Usually this means he'll grab one measly Kleenex and only succeed in smearing the mess around even more. Smile sweetly and thank him for his efforts, but by all means, feel free to reach over and grab a good wad of tissue and finish the job yourself.

If you are using condoms, needless to say, he's responsible for tying it up and chucking it afterwards.

Post-coital Protocol

Boys aren't the only ones who are eager to nod off after the act. Busy modern gals need their beauty sleep too. And not all women want to cuddle. So as long as both parties' needs are taken care of, and you've offered either a kiss or a "Thank

Quickie

According to Alfred Henry Tyrer in his 1936 book, *Sex, Marriage and Birth Control*, condoms are "the wife's responsibility." In preparation for sex, wives were supposed to dry the thing inside and out by "patting it gently between the folds of a fine linen cloth or handkerchief." Finally, she was to powder both sides with talcum powder or cornstarch.

you, that was lovely/awesome/mindblowing," nodding off in each other's arms is perfectly acceptable. Especially if it's five a.m. and you have to get up at six.

If your orgasm was one of those ones that leave your legs rubbery and your ability to speak impaired, some quiet spooning time is definitely required—until a limb falls asleep and you both finally give in, curl into fetal positions and pass out.

That said, you can't underestimate good afterplay. It's a great time to get to know someone better ("So, what was your name again?") or to put you back in touch with someone you already know pretty well. The fact that you've just locked body parts does tend to make you feel closer. And that post-sex grogginess is a bit like being drunk—you're more open and apt to spill your guts. But, as when drunk, it's best to avoid the really heavy topics.

There are things that happen in the dark between two people that make everything that happens in the light seem all right.

—Erica Jong, author

Chapter Four

AWKWARD MOMENTS

The Penile Code

Jumping the gun

Boys who ejaculate quickly tend to be, um, overly sensitive about the topic. Since women rarely have this problem, we sometimes have a hard time knowing how to handle a "preemie." Personally, I think premature ejaculation is in the eye of the beholder. When you think about it, a guy's ejaculation is only "premature" if it happens before either of you want it to. (That's why polite, modern folk prefer to now call it "rapid ejaculation.") I also get a little annoyed at those techniques designed to lessen sensation so guys can last longer. I'd rather have him focus on me and how good it all feels and enjoy a nice quick, feisty orgasm than have him last all night long thinking about his grandma or baseball statistics.

Luckily, therapists are smartening up and have realized the better way to get a guy to last longer is to actually increase rather than decrease his focus on sensation. And this is where you can help. Next time, rather than poke fun at your partner's lack of stamina (yes, "Wow, you came already" is bad etiquette), tell him to make you aware of when he feels he is about to come, then stop stimulation just before he comes. You can even give him a squeeze just below the glans of his penis until the feeling of impending orgasm dies off. Then start again and do the same thing. The more he does this and becomes aware of his bodily sensations, the more chance he has of delaying his orgasm. It's like building a muscle. And it's a much more polite way to deal with an overly enthusiastic young lad.

Bedtime Story

"My girlfriend and I were having sex, and soon after I entered her, I could feel myself ready to come. I was trying to hold off by stopping, starting and squeezing when, suddenly—Bam!—I got two vicious cramps in the backs of my upper legs. I nearly passed out, the pain was so excruciating. As I fell back off of her (and nearly off the bed), I completely lost focus on my other problem and promptly found myself having an orgasm! In between cries of pain and complete exasperation, I was howling with laughter. I don't think she was amused." **(Andrew, 29)**

A lasting problem

While we applaud stamina in a guy much more than we celebrate premature ejaculation, you still need to be sensitive in this situation. "For God's sake, are you ever going to come, dude?" is plain rude. Instead, talk to your guy. Find out if he takes this long to come when he masturbates. If not, have him masturbate for you and see if you can learn some of his tricks.

There may be psychological reasons he has a hard time reaching orgasm. Some guys carry heavy-duty guilt as a result of religious upbringing. Some guys can't come because of a fear of pregnancy. Find out if he has had this problem with other women. Does he take any prescription or non-prescription drugs? That could be part of the problem as well. Gently encourage your man to let you know if there are ways he'd like to be touched that would get him more aroused. It also might be nice to take the focus off orgasm altogether for a while—the more pressure he feels to come, the more difficult it can be. We know all about that, right girls?

Profile: The Marathon Man

You know the guy. He's pumping away, sweating, knees raw. The expression on his face is definitely not conveying pleasure—it looks more like he's bench-pressing two hundred pounds. That's about the point I put him in a leg hold and gently whisper "sloooow dowwwn."

If he's not enjoying it, I have to presume he's doing it because he thinks that's what he's supposed to do—or, worse yet—what I want. Well, he's not, and I don't.

What ever happened to quality, not quantity? I don't know if it stood a chance as an official Olympic sport for men, but somewhere along the line male endurance became a major goal in sexual intercourse. However it happened, we've now become obsessed with training men to last all night long. Books and manuals abound with tips on how to keep going till she's raw and chafed: use the squeeze technique, try the stop-start technique, wear double condoms, numb it with cream, try different positions, develop your PC muscles.

Sometimes we just want you to come already!

Besides, there is absolutely no rule that says once it's in, it has to stay there. And I'd take three minutes of the old in-out stretched out over a period of one hour—with a bunch of other stuff in between—over thirty minutes of straight humping any day.

Bedtime Story

"When my wife and I were engaged, she was still living with her parents. One afternoon, when her parents weren't home, we started having sex in her bedroom. I was really enjoying how expressive my girlfriend was being, but it seems her dog—a little silky terrier—wasn't and thought I was attacking her master. I suddenly felt a sharp pain in my ass when her dog bit me. My fiancée initially thought I was having an enjoyable orgasm until she realized what had happened. Her parents had come home and heard the dog yapping and me yelling. The bedroom door swung open as I was standing above my fiancée, nude, rubbing my ass and cussing up a storm. The dog was jumping up and down, yapping away, and my wife-to-be was laughing so hard tears were running down her face." **(Derrick, 40)**

Past Protocol

"[When it comes to temporary impotence] the wise and tactful wife may be the best of all physicians." (Source: Rev. Alfred Henry Tyrer, *Sex, Marriage and Birth Control*)

Losing it

You're having sex with your guy. Then, voom, something takes the wind out of his sails and he loses his erection. "It can happen," you think. "No biggie." And it's true. It's perfectly normal for a guy's pecker to occasionally lose its verve. Though it may act like it sometimes, it's not a machine with an on-off switch. Stress, fatigue and too much booze in one night can all put a wilt in his willy. Sadly, a guy's manhood is so tied in to the strength of his erection that if he loses it once, the sheer nervousness about losing it again can make him limp. It

Quickie

The term "impotent" is no longer considered polite. The accepted term these days is "erectile dysfunction."

becomes a touchy subject. Which is why responding with "Honey, why don't you get your ass to a doctor for some Viagra so you can have a decent erection for once?" isn't a good idea. Instead, turn up the compassion and coo, "That's okay, honey, it happens to all guys at some point" (it doesn't matter if it's true) in your best attempt to stop his ego from also deflating. Then run to your girlfriends and find out if this has ever happened to them and ask what they did about it. It's not disrespectful—that's what girlfriends are for.

Clearly, if the problem is ongoing, you need to talk openly with your partner about it. Reassure him that you're not bothered by it (even if you are, it won't help matters by saying so), and let him know that you'll work on the problem together. The trick is not to worsen things by putting more pressure on the poor guy. If he's still having erections outside of intercourse—for example, during masturbation—or he wakes up with a hard-on, the problem is clearly psychological, not mechanical. It'll take time to work out, so this is where you must be patient, supportive and understanding.

You could try a little jump-start from our little blue friend. I'm not a big fan of medicating sexual problems, but I know a guy who was having trouble achieving an erection during sex even though he still managed to get hard at other times. He took Viagra just a few times and it was enough to get him back on his game.

If that doesn't help and things don't change within six months, it might be time to seek some professional help.

Crimes of Passion

I can't believe you said that!

Good communication, as we all know, is the cornerstone of good sex. Inappropriate communication, on the other hand, can really kill the mood.

Things that should never be uttered in bed to a man

- Is it in yet?
- Funny, I had no problem coming with my last boyfriend.
- You don't mind if I just lie here while you do that, do you?
- You woke me up for that?
- Did you know the ceiling needs painting?
- Did I remember to take my pill?

Things that should never be uttered in bed to a woman

- It's cool how the dimples in your butt ripple when the light hits them a certain way.
- Did you come? (If you have to ask, we didn't, okay?)
- Wow, it's really roomy in there.
- Did I mention the video camera?
- Try breathing through your nose.
- It's nice being in bed with a woman I don't have to inflate!
- How long do you plan to be "almost there"?

Things that should never be uttered in bed to either sex

- But everybody looks funny naked!
- On second thought, let's turn off the lights.
- Got any penicillin?

What the Canuck!

June 2002: Dr. Paul Federoff, co-director of the sexual behaviours clinic at the Royal Ottawa Hospital, identifies a bizarre new disorder, "sexsomnia": engaging in sexual behaviour while asleep. (Source: *Ottawa Citizen*)

- I thought you had the keys to the handcuffs!
- Perhaps you're just out of practice.

"But my name is Andrea!"

If you're into year two or three of the relationship and he says the wrong name, he'd better have a good excuse or a comfy couch. Early in the game, screaming the wrong name in the heat of passion is a little more excusable. It can even be funny. A clever comeback can help: "No, I said I'm *so* randy." Even if he doesn't believe you, your quick wit might charm him. I said *might*. It might not be a bad idea to follow this up by shouting his name ten times at the top of your lungs the next time you have sex.

Am I keeping you up?

Given the number of people who have written to me about this little problem, it seems that falling asleep during the act happens with alarming regularity. I've heard of sexual ennui, but this seems a little acute. However, should you find yourself having a little trouble staying awake due to extreme fatigue—or, more commonly it seems, extreme substance intake—the only thing you can really do is apologize profusely and have a laugh about it. I mean, what are you going to say? "Oh, honey, you relax me so much with that thing you do with your tongue, you put me right to sleep." That'll make him feel like a real stud! If your sex life is so boring that it's putting you to sleep, you certainly don't want to encourage more of the same.

I like the woman who wrote to me once and said that falling

asleep while a guy's going down on you, for example, means it doesn't count and you must insist he do it over again. Very cute, but a little cheeky given that you're the one who passed out. Better to apologize and offer to make it up to him the next morning when you're well rested.

It's not the men in my life that counts, it's the life in my men.

—Mae West, actress

The Numbers Game

Inevitably, someone will pop the question. Yes, I'm talking about the biggie: How many people have you slept with? You have to be prepared. Your answer will influence your future together, so it requires some heavy soul-searching. You have to weigh your options and consider the consequences.

If the interrogator happens to be the person lying in bed beside me, nine times out of ten, I'll lie. It's not that I'm either ashamed or proud of the number of people I've slept with, it's just that guys have a hard time hearing about it—even if they say they want to know. Besides, I'm not really lying. I'm just using the revised version of my number—the one most women use after the usual equations have been worked out:

- Right off the top, rule out anyone whose name you can't remember.
- Lop off any other meaningless one-night stands devoid of emotional attachment.
- Bad-sex casual encounters can go. You might as well write off a few of your bad-sex long-term relationships while you're at it.

Quickie

To find out if you are officially a slut, take your age, subtract 15 and multiply by 5. If the number of lovers you've had exceeds your answer, you are officially a slut. Congratulations.

- Good-sex encounters where the guy turned out to be a big jerk (didn't call, or called to see if your friend was seeing anyone)—gone.
- Regrettable encounters, like the drunken one with that guy at work who won't leave you alone now? Outta there.
- If you did everything but "it," you don't have to count it, but just remember that by discounting it you become directly responsible for upholding the old intercourse = sex equation.
- Be sure you're not counting any guys twice. For example, if you went back to sleeping with an old lover, only count him once. In fact, if you're truly concerned about keeping your numbers down, recycling past lovers isn't a bad idea. You still get to have lots of sex without affecting the final tally.
- Oh yeah, and since your first few sexual encounters are usually pretty disastrous, you're allowed to disqualify them and start counting from your first good sexual encounter. Considering that for a lot of us that doesn't happen until we're thirty-five, this one can do wonders to get that number down.

Perhaps not surprisingly, guys are more concerned with inflating their numbers. So when tallying the number of women they've slept with, they ignore all the rules we girls use and then add all the times they *almost* slept with someone.

You're Only Human

Foul play

Some will advise you to ignore inadvertent passing of wind during the act, but I just can't. It's too funny. Besides, having a chuckle about it will ease the embarrassment for both of you and ultimately make you more at ease with each other. Imagine that. Farting bringing you closer—it's so romantic. Say something like, "Wow, you're good—you knocked the wind right outta me," have a laugh and move on. Of course, if it's a real stinker, you might want to take a break and let the air clear before moving on.

Same goes for vaginal farts, which are a result of air being trapped in the vagina (often a result of a lot of intense thrusting). At least they don't smell. By the way, pussy farts aren't only caused by thrusting. With regular Kegel exercises (squeezing the muscle that stops your pee midstream), you can, um, blow away the girls at your next sleepover with your queef-on-demand talents!

Bedtime Story

"My guy and I had had a very long and extremely fun evening enjoying each others' bodies, and I was falling asleep as he was spooning me. Suddenly, I broke wind. It woke me out of my semi-sleep instantly, but I pretended to be asleep; his reaction was a very soft 'Oh!' as he hugged me closer, and I could hear him laughing. I knew at that instant he was the one for me. (He is now my husband.) How embarrassing. I have never told him I was awake." **(Anne, 39)**

The uninvited guest

You've just met someone at the bar and you're bleeding like a stuck pig. But you're always horniest when you're on your period, and you want to go home with the guy. When do you reveal that it's going to be "car-wreck sex"? When you're still flirting at the bar? Or when he's pulling the tampon string out with his teeth? I think it's best to, er, come clean early in the game. Once you've lured him in, try growling something like this in his ear: "I'd love to screw you silly, baby, but it might be a little messy, if you know what I mean. Of course, it doesn't bother me if it doesn't bother you."

Then toss an old towel underneath the two of you to save the sheets and enjoy the added natural lubrication. By the way, it goes without saying that condoms are a must during all casual sex, whatever the time of the month.

Bedtime Story

"My boyfriend wanted to try 69-ing, so one night when we were having sex in the back seat of his car, we tried it. A cop showed up and told us to move on. We found another spot and continued where we'd left off. Believe it or not, another cop showed up and sent us on our way. We decided to go home, and my boyfriend asked to use the bathroom when he dropped me off. We walked in, and I turned on the light. I looked at my boyfriend's face, and it was clear I had started my period while we were going down on each other. I was too embarrassed to say anything. He used the bathroom and left without saying a word. Neither of us ever mentioned it." **(Erica, 22)**

Stuck on you

Remember the good old days when kids used to get their braces stuck together? Well, these days, you're more in danger of getting your genital piercings stuck. If this happens, stay calm. And whatever you do, don't tug. Ideally, one of you can twist yourself down there to get a good look at what's going on and untangle you. If you're really hooked, however, you may have to call a sympathetic friend to see if they can come by and gently unhook you. I know it sounds a little weird, but that's what friends are for.

Quickie

In medieval times, some women mixed their menstrual blood into food or drink and gave it to their husbands to make them more attentive. But according to the rules for sexual conduct compiled by the German bishop Burchard of Worms in 1012, women who did so had to do penance for five years on legitimate holy days. (Source: Richard Zacks, *History Laid Bare*)

A girl can wait for the right man to come along, but in the meantime that still doesn't mean she can't have a wonderful time with all the wrong ones.

—**Cher,**
actress and singer

Chapter Five

FLINGS AND THINGS

One-night Wonders

In these days of monogamy-means-never-having-to-say-you're-HIV-positive morality, casual sex has taken a bum rap. The truth is, I'm not so sure we're necessarily having less of it as a result, maybe just feeling more guilty about it (and, one hopes, playing it a little safer).

There's a lot to be said for casual sex. I encourage women who want to get over their inner good girl to have some casual flings, if only to liberate themselves from the idea that

Quickie

In the Middle Ages, any deviation from the missionary position was considered illegal—as, eventually, was sex on any Sunday, Wednesday or Friday, during the 40 days before Easter, during the 40 days before Christmas and 3 days before a communion. (Source: Harriett Gilbert and Christine Roche, *A Women's History of Sex*)

sex has to be precious. (Oh, I know, so many of you think sex should be sacred, but trust me, coming from a generation of women who were raised to believe our entire reputation and future depended on whether we did it, some of us can stand to be a little less uptight about it.) After all, for guys, having sex just because you're randy has been perfectly acceptable since the dawn of time.

Still, despite its moniker, there are many not-so-casual things about casual sex. In fact, the etiquette surrounding casual sex is almost more complicated than for its monogamous cousin. So, what are the rules?

- Both parties must be upfront about what they're looking for, allowing either party to opt out if he or she wants something more.
- "No strings" really means "no strings," not "no strings until after we have sex and I decide I actually really like you and want to see you again." Yes, I know it happens, but if the feeling's not mutual, you have to back off.
- "Casual" does not mean "cruel and insensitive." You can be direct and honest about not wanting to see the person again, but don't completely dismiss what went on between you.

Charm his pants off

So you've conquered your inner good girl and are now in hot pursuit of some no-strings nookie. But how does one go about finding some? It's rather indelicate to walk up to some person you fancy in a bar and say, "Hey you, I'm looking to have sex with someone tonight. You game?" A more civilized, and likely more effective way, would be as follows:

1. Find your target and move in.
2. Flirt. (I'm not going to tell you how. You have no business having one-night stands if you don't know how to flirt.)
3. If things are going well, let him know you'd like to exchange more than clever banter. A lot of guys have told me they're never sure when a woman's hitting on them, so don't be too subtle. A kick on the shin might be going a little too far. A well-timed lingering of your hand on his upper arm with a longer-than-usual look into his eyes should do the trick.
4. Now's the time to find out if he's game for a strictly recreational romp. Be direct and make your conditions clear so he can decide if he's on the same page.
5. Once he's on board, decide whose place you're going to. I like to go to mine because I can kick him out when I'm ready.

A word of caution: obviously, there are safety issues involved in going home with a complete stranger. It's a good idea to let friends know you're going home with someone and where you'll be. That way, if your one-night stand turns out to be an axe murderer, your friends will know where to find the body parts.

Indecent proposals

If you're being pestered to sleep with a guy you're not interested in, there is no protocol for politeness. If he can't take no for an answer and has decided that no means maybe, a little rudeness is in order. Walking away is the most dignified response, but if he is being a real jerk—and especially if he is being a drunken jerk—toss him a stop-him-in-his-tracks line. My current favourite comes from possibly the best good/bad movie of all time: *Swept Away* (the one with Madonna, not the original). My girlfriends and I use this line whenever we can, just because it's so over-the-top. In the movie, Madonna is a snooty socialite who is trying to put a measly, but handsome, deckhand in his place. The line? "I'd rather fuck a pig than kiss you, monkey boy!" Try it sometime. If just for your own amusement.

There's got to be a morning after

What is the protocol for the morning after a one-night stand? Do you share your toothbrush? Exchange phone numbers? Let's be honest: no one's going to be calling anyone. And you both have morning-after booze breath strong enough to peel paint. Lose the pretence. A simple, "Thanks, that was fun, nice to meetcha, take care," will suffice. Throw in a hug if you simply can't be that nonchalant.

If you don't want him there in the morning—the old half-night stand I like to call it—be upfront. No one wants to shag and then find out they're being turfed out into the cold, dark night. You could hang a "Breakfast Not Included" sign over the bed, but I think laying out the rules beforehand is much more polite. Tell your playmate you'd love to have sex but you're not up for a sleepover. You've got an early morning ahead, whatever. He will appreciate your honesty. If he doesn't, you'd best find out now.

And you would be . . .

C'mon, admit it, it's happened at least once in your life. Or if it hasn't, it's happened to someone you know. You rouse, semi-conscious, pry open your unbearably heavy eyelids and, over the pounding of your head, you hear the faint breathing of someone sleeping beside you. You turn your head slowly. Tom? No. Timothy? Tad? Shit, you can't remember. Fortunately, he is still asleep, so you lean out of bed and quickly scan the scattering of garments for a wallet so you can check his ID. Too late—your bedmate stirs and rolls over with a sly grin on his face. And he addresses you by name.

It's hard to think on your feet when you're horizontal, but you haven't been caught out . . . yet. You may have forgotten his name, but remember your manners. It would be disrespectful to someone you've clearly been intimate with to say "Nice getting naked together—and you would be?" Instead, proceed with caution and try one of these tactics:

- *Be honest.* Simply fess up and say, "You know what, I don't do this on a regular basis, but I was really drunk and I'm embarrassed to say I can't remember your name." The person will either laugh or be totally insulted. But, hey, what are the chances you're going to see him again, anyway?

- *Be sneaky.* Get him to write down his name and phone number. This does mean he might actually expect you to call.
- *Be clever.* Ask him how he spells his name. Of course, this only works if he has an unusual name. If his name happens to be "Bob," you'll be in trouble. "Oh, I have a friend who spells it B-a-w-b" is a little suspect.
- *Be creative.* Don't worry about what his name is. Do what my girlfriends and I do. Once you're rid of him, assign him a nickname based on the situation or something about him. At least your girlfriends will know whom you're talking about. Let's see, there was Ferret Boy (looked like a ferret, don't ask), Bagel Boy (worked in a bagel shop), Bookstore Boy—you get the idea.

The silent escape

You wake up. It's early. He is still happily snoring away next to you. You decide you have to leave . . . now! Should you leave a thank-you note? If you had a nice time, why not? Of course, what if the sex was bad? Do you leave a sympathy note? I think not.

If you feel, as I do, that dining and dashing is in poor taste, intercourse surely warrants a quick peck on the forehead before you leave. No need to loll about sipping cappuccino, reading the paper and discussing your lack of future together, but casual sex doesn't have to be uncivilized. If you really don't want to wake him, at least leave a note. But, ideally, you should gently jostle him awake, make a little small talk, crack a few jokes about what just happened—and then dash.

Don't I know you from somewhere?

Of course, it's all fun and games until you run into your one-night stand on the street. It's one thing to get butt-naked with a complete stranger and screw him silly, but it's quite another to see him in broad daylight, fully clothed, functioning in the real world. You'll likely have a tremendous urge to bend over and tie your shoe or slip a grocery bag over your head to avoid the awkward casual-sex follow-up. These are the moments that truly test a girl's mettle, but be polite and quickly neutralize the situation. Here are a few ways to handle yourself with dignity and tact:

- *Be funny:* "Sorry, I didn't recognize you with all your clothes on."
- *Be coy:* Shoot him a sly, knowing smile, combined with a casual, "Hi there, how's it going? Nice sleeping with you."
- *Be clever:* "Excuse me, you look exactly like someone I've slept with."
- *Be honest:* "I hope you don't feel too awkward about running into me. It was bound to happen."
- *Be polite:* "Can I buy you a drink? I promise not to take advantage of you—unless you insist."

I'll call you. No, really, I will

Sometimes you want a one-night stand to turn into a two-night stand, or even a three-night stand or, heaven forbid, a relationship. If you've had a change of heart, are you allowed to renege on your "one-night stand" position and ask to see the person again?

Be careful with this one. Because while you may be sweet on your bed buddy, he might still be in casual-sex mode and not interested in anything more. If you express a desire for a more lasting relationship, his reaction may make your heart sink and your idiot meter rise. Don't beat yourself up. Sometimes we surprise ourselves and get attached when we don't mean to. Attraction is unpredictable that way.

People often respond poorly when taken off guard, but that doesn't mean you should respond in kind. Get out of it with grace. Be honest with him. Tell him that you're disappointed, but that it's okay. This will make you seem very cool, and might even make him second-guess his decision. Okay, that's unlikely, but at least you're being straightforward—and leaving with your dignity intact. The relationship was meant to be casual, so overreacting would be out of line.

If the situations are reversed and your one-night stand suddenly wants more when you don't, remember your manners: "I really had a great time, and you're a great person, but it's just not there for me in the same way." Hey, we're grownups. We can handle it. A sobering moment of truth is far better than stringing him along because you're too cowardly to be honest.

One-night stand emergency kit

If you're heading out for a night on the town and you have even the faintest inkling that you're in for some action, here are a few things to toss into your bag before you head out the door. Just in case.

- *Travel-size toothpaste and toothbrush.* You don't want to use his, and the old toothpaste-on-the-finger trick won't get the sweaters off your teeth.
- *Travel-size moisturizer.* Because you know he's gonna have some crappy soap in his bathroom that will leave your skin so tight you'll feel like you've had a facelift.
- *A clean T-shirt.* Roll it up, toss it in your bag and hope tomorrow is casual Friday. If it isn't, just tell people at the office you've been super busy and lost track of what day it is.
- *Elastic or hair clip.* He's unlikely to have a hairdryer and a large round brush.
- *Shades.* I know, I know, it was dark when you went out, but man, that sun is bright this morning, isn't it?
- *Condoms.* A gal should never travel without. You can also fill one with ice and use it as a cold pack to nurse your blinding hangover headache on your "walk of shame" to home or work.
- *A good exit line.* This way you won't be tempted to say "I'll call you" when you know you won't. Something along the lines of, "Thanks, I had a great time. I'll let myself out. Have a good life" will do.

Fling Flare

The fling lies somewhere between a one-night stand and a relationship. The beauty of a fling is that you get to enjoy all the benefits of a new relationship without having all the

Quickie

It is known that public ceremonies of sexual intercourse took place in China in the first century AD, often at certain phases of the moon. This despite the fact that merely kissing in public was considered taboo. (Source: Sarah Dening, *The Mythology of Sex*)

emotional heavy-lifting of something long term. And you don't have to meet his parents. It can be pure bliss, and the sex is usually better than that in a one-night stand because you're more connected, yet it doesn't get predictable, as relationship sex sometimes can. Sleep is unimportant because you're both totally fascinated by everything you have to say to each other, and when you're not, it's okay because you always want to have more sex.

Flings can be a wonderful way to pull yourself out of the emotional ties of a previous relationship. Or they can simply be a wonderful adventure while travelling or a way to escape life for a while. But you have to be careful not to be fooled by the intensity of a fling and mistake it for a deeper connection. Yes, I know you feel wonderful right now. But it will end, and if you don't follow these rules of conduct, you'll get flung right into a pit of emotional despair. These are here for your protection!

- No expectations allowed. Remember, this is not Mr. Right, just Mr. Right Now.
- Don't mistake lust for love.
- Always be aware that there are emotional limitations to this "relationship."
- Don't say "I love you" after Day 2.
- When a fling ends (and it always does), let it go gracefully. No quitting your job, giving up your apartment and following him to the other side of the world. I mean it!

Booty-call Basics

Not a one-night stand, a fling or a relationship, the booty call can be a convenient way to get some regular action between relationships without all the muss and fuss of picking up strangers in bars. When you want sex, you simply call up booty-call boy and, if he's available, you get together. Sounds brilliant, doesn't it? It can be, but this kind of casual sex is often like a warm glass of milk—it can be comforting, but if it's left too long it eventually sours. Here's the 411 on booty-call etiquette:

- *Rule #1:* Respect the system. The key to a successful booty-call relationship is to understand the terms. These arrangements are like a delicate ecosystem. Start mucking with the arrangement, and you're usually asking for trouble. If one of you has missed the point—or conveniently forgotten it—you'd best get out of there.
- *Rule #2:* Establish a special code or sign to avoid misunderstandings. If you're out flirting with another guy, and your booty-call buddy happens to show up, have a hand signal or code word that lets him know you're closed for business with him tonight.
- *Rule #3:* Booty calls are not guaranteed. You can't feel rejected if you're out with your booty call and they a) don't want to go home with you or b) want to go home with someone else.
- *Rule #4:* Limit the drunken booty calls. It's to be expected in a purely sex-driven relationship that occasionally

you're all liquored up and decide you'd like to get some. But calling drunk at three a.m. on a regular basis is rude and abuses your booty-call privileges.

- *Rule #5:* Don't fill booty-call buddies in on your dating activities unless you plan on getting serious with someone else. Why spoil a good thing before you have to?
- *Rule #6:* Booty calls usually have a shelf life. No sulking when your buddy gets a real date. This is the reason so many booty-call relationships go awry. It's all fun and games until someone finds themselves some more serious action.

Considering all the rules, why bother? Because it gets bloody tiresome trying to find the kind of relationship we know we deserve. Sometimes we just need something familiar to get us through the night.

Bedtime Story

"A friend and I got drunk and ended up fooling around. I passed out, and he headed to the bathroom. The door automatically shut behind him, locking him in. There he was: naked, banging on the door and yelling at the top of his lungs for me to let him out. I didn't hear a thing. The upstairs neighbour—the landlord's daughter—who was unable to get me to answer the phone—thought I was being attacked and called the cops. She let the cops in, and they let my friend—who had found a small hand towel to wrap around himself—

out of the bathroom. I slept through it all, and my friend insisted the cops not wake me as I had an early morning the next day. After a perfunctory check that he hadn't actually killed me or anything, they left. I didn't believe any of this had happened until I heard my neighbour's phone messages the next morning. How humiliating to run into her after that!" **(Karen, 39)**

Rebounding Rules

I honestly think the government should pass legislation that forces those of us who are newly single to wear a sign on our foreheads that reads: "I'm on the rebound." Much like those nasty surgeon general warnings on cigarette packs. It's only responsible to inform the public of the potential risks involved. We all know that rebounders are hazardous to our health. That's because a rebounder isn't looking for love, a rebounder is looking for pain relief, validation and something to stave off the horrible fear that they will die bitter and alone.

Getting involved with a rebounder is a proceed-at-your-own-risk venture, but it's only fair that those on the rebound respect some rebound relationship rules. As a responsible rebounder, you should:

- Avoid packing all your shit from the last relationship and dumping it on the doorstep of the first person that takes pity on you—I mean, agrees to go out with you.
- Never drag replacement material—ahem, new people—

into unresolved drama with your ex. The new guy should not be subject to jealous rages and flying chairs if you happen to run into the ex on the street.

- Limit sexual activity to flirting and crushes for the first few months. As long as no one gets naked, there is less risk of anyone getting hurt. Flirting gives you that superficial I've-still-got-it confidence that helps you get over an ex, and no one has to dodge flying chairs.

Ex Sex

While I try to make a habit of becoming friends with my exes (I consider it the minimum return on my investment), it can sometimes be tricky. There are no set rules on how much time must pass before this is possible. But a loose mathematical equation—something like the ugliness of the breakup divided by the combined level of maturity—should equal how long you have to wait before you attempt friendship.

You know what happens when you try to pretend you're over it too soon. It starts on the phone, and then you agree to get together. Once face to face, chemistry takes over and you fall for some crap about things being different. It's easy to get sucked in by familiarity and a selective memory. You just slip on your rose-coloured glasses and convince yourself it wasn't so bad—especially if there's no one else waiting in the wings. Then your sex drive butts in on the conversation, and the next thing you know it's the morning and you're making coffee for two and suffering a major emotional hangover from falling off the wagon.

Having sex with an ex isn't without its charms, mind you. "Ex sex" can be a very convenient temporary way of getting some action. But the sex isn't usually as good as you imagined it would be. Not just because you're often soused, but because reality has a hard time living up to fantasy, and you usually can't recreate what you once had.

If you do decide to have sex with an ex, there are a few things to keep in mind:

- Don't sleep with him in the hopes of getting back together.
- Avoid calling him at three a.m. if you know he has a girlfriend. Same goes for showing up on his doorstep unannounced.
- No more than three booty calls after the breakup (more than that means you're having trouble moving on and you need to reconsider why you broke up in the first place).
- And remember: he hasn't changed.

My Best Friend's Guy

With all the people out there, why do so many of us feel the need to recycle our friends' dates? Life is not a TV soap opera where everyone has to sleep with someone else's ex

Past Protocol

"Never, never, NEVER, steal a man from another girl (that is, if you can help it!)." (Source: Roy Lee Sherman and Lillian Preston, *Sex-Life of the Career Girl*, 1965)

because there are only so many characters to go around. Dating a friend's ex is like eating off someone else's plate. Order your own damn food!

And I don't care if she dumped him. I still think it's in poor taste to go after a friend's ex. After all, do you think she dumped the guy so she could have him back in her face, and schtuping one of her girlfriends to boot?

There are few guys worth losing a friend over, which is usually what happens if you sleep with her ex. (For the record, it's also extremely ill-mannered for an ex to sleep with any of your friends after the two of you break up.) But let's be realistic. While I think it's only considerate to at least try to fish in another pond after a breakup, we can't always (or don't always want to) control who we fall in love with or even fall into bed with. Given how tough it is to meet people, the folks we already know—even if they did date our best friend—often get pushed to the front of the line.

If you're hell-bent on dating a friend's ex, there are more tactful ways to go about it than getting caught shagging in the linen closet at a party. Start by asking yourself the following questions:

- How long has it been since the breakup? Obviously, the longer it's been, the more she's over it, and—in theory, at least—the more acceptable it is for you to move in.
- How nasty was the breakup? The nastier it was, the less chance there is she'll want the guy anywhere near her life, and since you're in her life, she might not take kindly to the two of you dating.

- Are you willing to risk losing a friend by dating her ex?
- If the attraction is purely physical, is a one-night romp worth jeopardizing a friendship?
- Would you be willing to first talk to your friend about your attraction to her ex and see how she feels about it? Maybe she'll be cool with it (it does happen), and you can follow your heart guilt-free.

Profile: The Tease

I have a male friend whose best friend's girlfriend used to undress in front of him or come into his room in her underwear at night "to chat." It drove him crazy. I know it's fun to tease, but this is crude and insensitive behaviour. Men can be teases too—though, oddly, terms like "cunt-tease" or "pussy-tease" haven't made it into the popular vernacular. Ever have a guy flirt like crazy with you, then you find out later he has a girlfriend? Maddening, isn't it? It's okay to flirt as long as you don't start promising things you can't deliver. It's a thrill to make someone wait for it, even to make them crazy with wanting, but only if you're in a position to follow through at some point. Teasing to satisfy your own ego, as fun as it is for you, is in poor taste.

You've Got Mail

Email has forever changed the way we conduct ourselves in the world of love and lust. These days, you're more likely to stumble home with a barely legible email address scrawled on a matchbook than with a phone number. "Will he call?" has turned into "Will he email?"

Email has made us bolder in our romantic pursuits. While we might not have the guts to tell someone in person how much the outfit they're wearing tonight turns us on, back home alone at two a.m., our confidence boosted by caffeine or alcohol and our face safely hidden behind our computer screen, we can say things we ordinarily wouldn't.

Email has also changed how we flirt. "Simply throwing an X and O at the bottom of a friendly email can help fan the flames of a potential relationship by letting the person know that you like them that little bit extra," explains a male friend of mine. It can also cause confusion, as we find ourselves analyzing every bit of punctuation and turn of phrase. Does the XO mean he likes me, or is he just being overly friendly?

A friend of mine—who says she could have published and sold some of the emails she shared with a long-distance lover—insists email sex is more shocking and titillating than phone sex. "I think that words on a page can leave so much more to the imagination, whereas when you hear them spoken, it flattens and limits them to the meaning the person speaking them intends," she says.

Certainly, some of the things we say in an effort to sound sexy can come off as absurd or even comical. But in emails, somehow, all that coarse or dorky stuff just seems hot. Part of the reason, believes a female friend of mine, is that we're more fearless online. "Stuff that we would never deem fit to put on paper seems fair game online. I've found that in my online sexual encounters things can get very explicit, very quickly," she says. "And ultra-raunchy stuff that, to me, would sound corny or clichéd in 'real life' can be really exciting online." But once again you want to be careful. If you're dealing with an unethical or slightly unscrupulous person, your dirtiest thoughts could end up being forwarded all over the place.

Chatting politely

The Internet has revolutionized the way we think about—and express—our sexuality. Now we can sit in the comfort of our own homes in our smelly slippers and greasy hair and pretend to be glamorous sexual beings, expressing our ultimate sexual desires to complete strangers. No, it's a good thing, really. Well, okay, it's kind of a good thing, at least for people who are shy and who otherwise have a hard time meeting people and getting any. Also, how else would you find like-minded people who get off sexually by dumping spaghetti on their heads? The Internet allows us to skip the hassles of getting dressed, going out to a bar, and picking someone up. Now you can simply shop online, whether you're looking for something in a casual on- or off-line sexual encounter.

But despite its ability to bring people together for whatever sexual reasons, the anonymity of the Internet raises some specific safety issues as well as making it a breeding ground for atrociously inappropriate behaviour. To that end, here is a beginner's guide to some basic etiquette when chatting online:

What the Canuck!

December 2003: Sharon Smith, 48, the first female mayor of the mountain resort town of Houston, British Columbia, was asked to step down when naked photos of her were downloaded off her home computer and circulated worldwide on the Internet. Smith said the pictures—one showing her grinning naked in her official black leather chair wearing only her ceremonial chain—were taken by her husband to celebrate her election. (Source: Canadian Press)

- Mind your manners. Just because you can't see the person, it doesn't give you permission to morph into a vulgarian.
- Pick screen names appropriate to the venue. "Buttslammer" might not go over so well on a Christian singles site, for example.
- Don't lie about yourself. At least not too much. Especially if you hope to meet this person one day. If you embellish your physical characteristics, you risk alienating your new friend—and embarrassing yourself—when the fantasy you've created doesn't match reality.
- Don't demand personal details from someone right off the bat. Just as in off-line life, basic conversation etiquette should be honoured.
- DON'T YELL.
- Don't get sexual in a chat room where it's not welcome.
- Feel free to report inappropriate behaviour to the website administrator.
- Don't spy on people in private "conversation."
- Be aware that most adult personals or chat sites are monitored in some way, so be careful what details you reveal about yourself.
- If someone responds to your adult personal, and you're not interested, at least send a polite "thanks, but no thanks" email to let him know you got his message so he can move on.
- If someone blows you off, move on. No cyber stalking.
- Think twice before sending anyone sexy pics. You never know where they could end up.

- If you're using webcams and things are getting sexy, know that the person watching you can save the images on to his computer and then post them.
- Don't give out personal information to strangers you meet online.
- If you decide to meet someone off-line, meet in a public place.

Chat code

BF: Boyfriend
CYAL8R: See ya later
EG: Evil grin
GF: Girlfriend
H&K: Hug and kiss
KIT: Keep in touch
KOC: Kiss on cheek
KOL: Kiss on lips
LOL: Laughing out loud
LY: Love ya
PM: Private message
SO: Significant other
TOY: Thinking of you

Condoms should be marketed in three sizes: jumbo, colossal and super colossal, so guys don't have to go in and ask for the small.

—**Barbara Seaman, author**

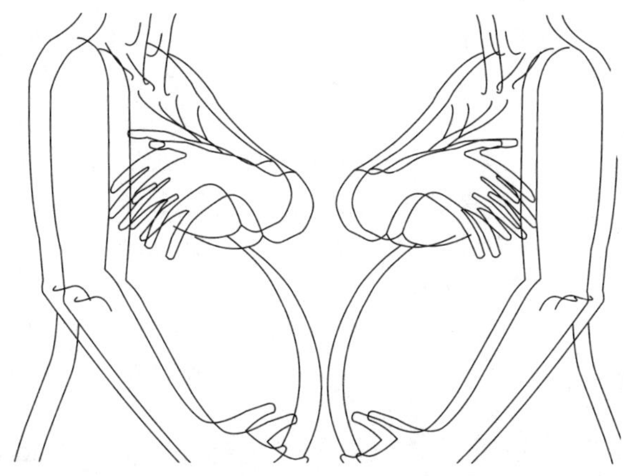

Chapter Six

REALITY CHECK

The P's and Q's of STIs*

STIs are such a riot, aren't they? Never mind the obvious anxiety they cause as a health problem, the stigma they carry is almost worse. You know how it is: a lover tells you he has herpes, and, instead of thanking him for letting you know, you think, "Yuck!" and can't help but wonder where he's been.

* The term "sexually transmitted disease," or STD, is no longer considered appropriate in progressive circles. The preferred term these days is "sexually transmitted infection," or STI, since these bugs are not technically diseases but infections.

Quickie

It is not just discourteous, it is illegal in Canada to knowingly pass on a STI.

So, out of fear of rejection and shame, people—even nice, normally considerate ones—avoid telling their lovers altogether.

It is a gross breach of etiquette to neglect to inform a lover of any sexual health concerns. It is only fair to give him the choice of whether to put himself at risk. That said, how do you bring it up? "Hey, I have herpes. You still wanna come home with me?" isn't going to cut it. You also don't want to wait until you are in the throes of ecstasy to pull out your sexual health file. Timing is everything.

The best approach is to say something like, "Before we sleep together, I just want to let you know that many years ago I contracted herpes/venereal warts/chlamydia. It's not as serious as it sounds, and I haven't had an outbreak in weeks/months/years. I just want to let you know so you can make your own choice. Here are the risks if we use a condom . . ."

This means you have to educate yourself about the risks of your particular STI(s) so you can be straightforward and confident with your partner. People usually appreciate honesty. Your partner may have a few STIs up his sleeve too. If he freaks, you might want to consider what you're doing with the lunkhead.

A few uninformed people will react negatively no matter what you say or how you say it. Remember, these people are the exception, not the rule. If a partner decides not to pursue a relationship with you because you have a STI, it's best to know this now. There are many people who will be attracted to you for who you are—with or without bugs.

Bedtime Story

"I had just moved to a new city, in part to escape a bad relationship. One day at work, I went to the bathroom to relieve an incessant itch and ended up scratching a little critter out of my pubes. I realized I had crabs. Years later, when I saw the guy I suspected had given them to me, I thanked him for the lovely going-away present. He said, 'Oh, you mean the chlamydia?' I couldn't believe it. Two for the price of one. And even worse, he told me his new girlfriend got chlamydia from him too, and she told everyone it came from me!" **(Andrea, 32)**

The blame game

Ah, the STI source—always good for a little finger-pointing, shame, guilt and embarrassment. Of course, it's always the other person's fault.

Rule #1 when your partner discovers he has an STI: Don't assign blame. People come up with all kinds of stories about how they got infected ("I was playing with my friend's goldfish, and, uh . . ."), which lead to misinformation about how STIs are transmitted. Some STIs—viruses like herpes or human papillomavirus, more commonly known as genital warts—can lie dormant in your system for years without you even knowing they're there. A doctor once told me a story about a nun who developed genital herpes at age eighty-five even though she swore she hadn't had sex since her teenage years. Rather than sitting

Quickie

The mother of all sexual health infections is HIV. Having to track down and notify everyone you've slept with can be overwhelming. Many AIDS counselling and referral services provide counsellors who will help the seropositive person identify who needs to be notified and assist in the process of informing them of their potential risk of infection.

around trying to place blame, get thee to a doctor and get the situation dealt with.

Disclosure decorum

If a partner isn't forthcoming about potential sexual health problems, is it proper to ask? Absolutely. You owe it to yourself. Just apply some tact and be sensitive to the scenario. It's perfectly acceptable to say to the person you are about to sleep with, "Hey, gorgeous, I'm really into having sex with you, and I really care about you and want you to be safe. I want you to know I don't have any sexual health problems that I know of [if you do, this would be a good time to disclose], and I want you to feel comfortable enough with me to let me know if there is anything I need to be aware of." The trick is to avoid any wording that sounds judgemental—and please, don't ever use the phrase "I'm clean." It reinforces the idea that people who've had the misfortune to contract an infection are dirty. Condoms can't protect you from all STIs, so if you're having sex, you're susceptible. Don't act like you're special.

Condom code

With so much to choose from, there's no excuse not to wear a raincoat. Condoms are made out of three types of materials:

Latex—The strongest and most common condom material. It is inexpensive and offers the most protection from STIs and pregnancy (90 percent to 96 percent effective). Not good

Profile: The Shrinker

After twenty-odd years of safer-sex education, condom demonstrations, and being beaten over the head with messages about protecting yourself and your partner, there are still guys whose willies wilt at the mere crinkle of a condom wrapper. You've heard him whine, "But I can't *feel* anything with a condom on." My response: "Well, you won't feel anything with it off, either, buddy, 'cause we won't be having sex." And you know what? Call me crazy, but I've even heard that guys can get it up more than once a round. FYI, a fresh erection requires a fresh condom. Now that condoms come in so many sizes, styles and thicknesses, no longer does The Shrinker have to shy away from tight-fitting, uncomfortable or overly thick condoms. There is nothing sexier than a man who has done his research and sports his favourite brand. There are no excuses. Refusing to wear a rubber is just stupid and rude.

for people with latex allergies, and will disintegrate if used with oil-based lubricants.

Lambskin—Actually made of sheep intestine. This is what condoms were made of before latex came along. While lambskin condoms will prevent pregnancy, they will not protect you from HIV and other STIs.

Polyurethane—Good for people who are allergic to latex. These are more expensive and are not as elastic as latex condoms (kind of like a thin sandwich bag), so they are more prone to breakage.

Quickie

In a LTR (long-term relationship), the cost of condoms and birth control should be shared by both partners.

Here are some other condom terms to help you out when you're confounded by all the choices available:

Female condom—A loose-fitting polyurethane sheath that lines the vagina, with soft rings at either end to keep it in place. More expensive than regular condoms and not unlike having a plastic bag in your vagina during sex.

Flavoured—Condoms with usually sickening flavours like tutti frutti and banana shake. These condoms are coated with sugar, corn syrup or other fructoses that can dramatically alter the pH of the vagina and set the stage for yeast infections. They are not recommended for vaginal or anal sex, but are okay for oral sex on men.

Lubricated—Most condoms are lubricated with a silicone- or water-based substance, making the condom easier to put on and more comfortable to use.

Nonoxynol-9—Some lubricated condoms contain the spermicide nonoxynol-9, intended for extra protection against pregnancy. However, nonoxynol-9 is a detergent that can cause irritation in the mucous membranes of the genitals, causing small sores that can increase the risk of HIV transmission.

Reservoir tip—The tip at the end of the condom that allows room for the semen when a man ejaculates.

Rubber rules

- Keep condoms within lunging distance of the bed (or in other strategic locations around the house if you like to move around).

- If he refuses to wear a condom, apply the same rule they do at fine eating establishments: Visitors without jackets will not be permitted entry. End of story.
- If he's self administering, let him get on with it. After all, he's probably a little more familiar with the equipment.
- If you want to impress him, put the condom in your mouth and slide it down. Or just use your hands and seductively roll down the rim to win!
- Check periodically to make sure the condom is still okay. If it breaks and he hasn't come yet, have him pull out and replace it. If you don't notice until it's too late, assess your risk for pregnancy. It's not a bad idea to keep some spermicide handy for just such an occasion so you can blast those suckers dead. If you're less certain of your cycle, get thee to a doctor and get a morning-after pill. And, yes, he should go with you.
- He's the one who has to hold it to pull out, so he might as well be polite and dispose of it as well. That is, tie a nice knot in it and throw it in the trash. We all know by now not to flush condoms down the toilet, right?

Personal taste

The jury is still out regarding the risks of oral sex without a condom or dental dam—a rectangular piece of latex you've probably seen at your dentist's office that can also be held over a woman's vulva or over the bum while oral sex is performed to protect against transmission of STIs and HIV. Don't be offended by a request to cover up—that's hardly fair since we expect the boys to wear their raincoats. As for suiting the

Past Protocol

"It is true that some men object strenuously to using condoms, but where a wife's health may be at stake no reasonable man will refuse to take advantage of so simple, and (if properly used) dependable a means." (Source: Rev. Alfred Henry Tyrer *Sex, Marriage and Birth Control*)

What the Canuck!

August 2003: Planned Parenthood, an organization that promotes birth control and sexual health, mails 15,000 condoms to addresses across Canada. The condoms are sent in envelopes marked with the words "It's hard to buy a condom when your uncle owns the only pharmacy in town," demonstrating the campaign organizers' goal to promote good communication about healthy sexuality. (Source: *Ottawa Citizen*)

boy up to go down on him, that's a personal choice. If you're not a big fan of sucking on Tupperware, you may decide to go bare. Or you can try flavoured condoms to sweeten the deal.

A Pregnant Pause

You're both hot and randy and he's about to slide on home, when suddenly he whispers gruffly in your ear, "You're on the pill, right, baby?" A perfect, yet frighteningly still common, example of how not to introduce the subject of birth control with a new lover. Never mind that even if you were on the pill, neither of you would be protected from STIs or HIV.

I am amazed at the number of adults—yes, I'm talking grownups, even well-informed university-educated ones—who say things to me like: "Oh, we're being careful," or, "I'm convinced I'm sterile," or that old classic, "I can't come with a condom on." Quite an example. And we're surprised the teen pregnancy rates are up.

Bedtime Story

"My boyfriend and I were having sex, and at one point he said, 'Where did the condom go?' We stopped to look for it, but couldn't find it anywhere in the room or in me. The next morning I took a shower, and after much poking and prodding I found it. It was pretty embarrassing to explain what had happened when I went to a clinic for the morning-after pill." **(Faith, 23)**

In case you've forgotten, that's what happens when you don't practise proper birth control—unplanned pregnancy. Which is fine if you're in a situation where you're both ready to have a kid and think you can handle it. But if you haven't even talked about it, if you don't even know whether he likes children, well, you might be wishing that you'd had that discussion about birth control a little earlier.

If you want to see this through, however, you need to decide if you would feel the same way if he wasn't involved. If he doesn't want to share this responsibility, you can't force him.

If you don't want to have a child right now and choose to have an abortion, don't think you can sneak off without him knowing. These kinds of secrets have a way of biting you in the ass later. And imagine how much more upset he will be if he finds out you were pregnant and had an abortion without telling him. He has the right to know, but he doesn't have the right to tell you not to have one. That is your choice.

What the Canuck!

March 2003: The Today Sponge contraceptive returns—8 years after being taken off the market due to the financial problems of its producers—and is made available through Canadian websites only. (Source: Associated Press)

There is one thing I would break up over, and that is if she caught me with another woman. I wouldn't stand for that.

—Steve Martin,
actor and comedian

Chapter Seven

THE ENDURANCE TEST

Finding the Same Frequency

Judging by the number of people who come to me wanting to know whether they're doing it enough, a lot of couples seem to be concerned that every other couple is getting way more action than they are. Let me assure you that plenty of people are just as stressed, tired, busy and uninspired as you when it comes to sex. Especially if you've been with the same person for a while and there are a few kids tossed into the mix. When it comes to frequency, there isn't a "normal" or "appropriate" number of times to be getting it on. Besides, as I always say, Quality, not quantity, people! I'd rather have mind-blowing, connected, meaningful sex once a month than a quick poke every night. Not that the occasional weeknight quickie isn't fun, but you get my point. Frequency is only an issue if one of you is not getting enough—or is getting too much. If you're both blissfully happy with a once-a-year romp, don't feel bad. Same goes if you're doing it every hour on the hour. As long as everyone's happy.

Initiation Rites

Remember when you couldn't keep your paws off each other? When you never thought about whose turn it was to initiate? All it took for sex to happen was for both of you to be within, well, pawing distance.

Once this stage passes, initiating sex can become as big an issue as who did the dishes or who last took out the trash. And it's not just guys complaining. You'll be pleased to hear, ladies, that we're entering a new phase of sexual liberation: Equal Opportunity Frustration. I am getting more and more letters from women who are annoyed that their men aren't the tigers they once were. Yes, we've come a long way, baby.

What's the protocol here? Who should initiate when you've been together for a long time? Ideally, you should be sharing initiation rites. Because if one person is always the initiator, he inevitably starts feeling resentful and she starts feeling pressured. Or vice versa. If you find one of you is always kick-starting sex, turn the tables once in a while and encourage the other person to take the lead.

When it comes to proper behaviour, however, it's not just a question of who initiates, but how you initiate:

- Just as we don't consider having a morning hard-on pressed into our backs the height of seduction, men might want us gals to be a little more imaginative than simply giving him a look and climbing on board. However, giving him a look and climbing on board is welcome on occasion.
- Because we're raised to think that guys want it any time, anywhere, women often feel rejected if we initiate and he's not into it. But guys can occasionally feel unsexy too. Occasionally, he may need time to get in the mood. No, really. After a hard day's work, a fella might like to be greeted with a nice glass of wine and a shoulder massage.
- On the other hand, some men need quiet time alone when they're feeling disconnected from their partner and their libido. Resist your temptation to ask him for the zillionth time, "What's wrong, honey?" He'll appreciate the space and will eventually come around.

Profile: The Sheet Stealer

It's mid-January, but you've had a steamy night and you've gently drifted off in your lover's arms only to wake up shivering and naked beside a human cocoon who has stolen all the sheets. As much as you'd like to unravel him like a Pillsbury Crescent Roll, be kind. He did do this in his sleep and—who knows?—maybe he was swarmed by a herd of butterflies as a child and has been scarred by a bizarre affliction to cocoon ever since.

Gently nudge your sweet nubbins, nuzzle up to his sleepy, tousled head and whisper sweetly into his ear: "You've got all the friggin' sheets, butthead, and if you don't give some back to me I'm never having sex with you again!"

Or, if it's chronic, keep some extra sheets beside the bed. Before you drift off, grab them and tuck them in around you. Hell, staple them to the bed if you must. Then he can steal away and you don't have to wake up a human Popsicle every night.

Passionately Speaking

Even if you're having sex an average of 2.6 times a week (no, I don't know what the "real" average is, so stop comparing!), you both initiate sex, and you have perfectly matched sex drives, having sex with the same person year after year gets, well, how can I put this delicately, dull. Sure, the sex is deeper and more meaningful (blah, blah, blah), but admit it, sometimes you yearn to recreate those lust-filled early days of throwing each other against walls and furniture because you just couldn't get enough. But when I get letters from people who are worried because they've been married for years and their sex life has lost its lustre, I think, Jeez, what's the big

Past Protocol

"Variety in sex technique, as in most other things in life (tea out in the garden, for instance), adds a certain spice that need not be refused for any reason known to common sense." (Source: Rev. Alfred Henry Tyrer, *Sex, Marriage and Birth Control*)

surprise there? I'd be more surprised if they were having sex with the same person for years on end and not getting bored once in a while.

In some respects, the intimacy that exists between two people in long-term relationships should make it easier to communicate sexual frustrations. However, the closer you are, the more you have at stake, which makes talking about sex scary. And while "You bore me, honey" may be honest, it's not the most polite or efficient way to turn up the heat in a long-term relationship. Instead, try these suggestions:

- *Create time.* After juggling work, kids, family, friends and the occasional load of laundry, a night in front of the TV or in bed sleeping is often more appealing than sex. At least once a week, put a lock on the door, tell the kids this is mommy and daddy's playtime and then, well, play.
- *Break the routine.* I know you've been doing this since high school—kissing; manipulation of breasts; hand in crotch and so on—but have you ever *really* explored the backs of his knees?
- *Speak up early in the game.* If the way he tweaks your nipples kind of annoyed you when you were first going out, it's going to make you want to "purple nurple" him until he screams for mercy by about year five. If you put more effort into getting to know each other sexually from day one, you stand a better chance of solving sexual problems later.

Quickie

According to Dr. David Schnarch, author of *Passionate Marriage*, only about 15% to 30% of couples open their eyes at all during sex, with roughly half of those folks closing them again during orgasm. As a result, argues Schnarch, the sex a lot of people experience within long-term relationships is more like mutual masturbation than making love (not that we've got anything against mutual masturbation). I know staring is considered rude, but Schnarch suggests one simple way to increase passion and feel more connected to your partner: try opening your eyes and looking at your partner during orgasm.

Past Protocol

"Do not grind your teeth in your sleep, thrash around with your clenched fists, or toss and twist so much that you wind the bedclothes into a tight cocoon around yourself, leaving your pillow-partner bare. . . . Remember what Emerson said: 'Good manners are made up of petty sacrifices.'" (Source: Dr. Ralph Y. Hopton and Anne Balliol, *Bed Manners: How to Bring Sunshine into Your Life*, 1942)

Profile: The Cuddler

You know the ones. You wake up with their limbs wrapped around you like octopus tentacles. In fact, you don't know how he hangs on, given the slippery layer of sweat that has formed between your naked limbs. Yet he clings like a drowning victim on the *Titanic*. Look, folks, there's cuddling and then there's suffocating your lover nightly by wrapping your body around him like flypaper. As much as we all love a little affection, some of us are also fond of breathing. A good cuddler knows her limits. It's fine to have some quiet spooning time after sex or to nestle into your lover's chest for some post-coital affection or simply to nuzzle a little before drifting off, even if no sex has occurred. But once sleep settles in, cuddling duties are off. The occasional squeeze of a hand while rolling over or the rub of a foot or arm is fine, but once you've spent an appropriate amount of time cuddling (to be negotiated between yourselves), you are both free to curl up in the fetal position or stretch out on your back with your arms above your head or whatever other weird position you have been sleeping in since you were warmly ensconced in your mother's womb.

Sextracurricular Activities

Honey, what's this?

So you've stumbled across his stack of porn magazines or you've discovered his extensive collection of porn videos. Hey, maybe it really will be "worth" something someday.

Perhaps he actually was surfing XXXmidgetporn .com for an article he was researching. (Heaven forbid anyone look at where I've surfed in the name of research.) Modern girls should hardly be shocked that—eep!—guys like porn. In fact, given that more and more porn is being produced for us (I'll call it erotica if it makes you feel better), most modern girls should have their own collection of the stuff by now.

Still, it can be jarring to find out your partner's a big old smut snaffler, especially if he's got a closet full of foot-fetish tapes and has never mentioned his taste for tootsies. Rather than freak out and parade him around the neighbourhood carrying a "Beware: I Am Freaky Pervert" sign, give him a break. He's a guy. Porn is a rite of passage for most men. It doesn't mean he doesn't get off on real-live sex with you.

As for stuff that seems a little bent, I'm sure you've got a few dirty little secrets of your own you'd rather he not discover. I think couples should be allowed to have their own private fantasies, even if some of them are a little twisted. As long as he's not doing anyone any harm and not actually screwing midgets behind your back—in reality or virtually—what's the harm? There's a big difference between fantasy and reality. If after all this, you simply can't live with this side of your partner, he'll have to decide what is more important to him: The midgets or you.

What the Canuck!

A study by Media Matrix showed that Canadians rank first in the world when it comes to the amount of time spent downloading porn on the Internet. One-third of our online viewing is dedicated to porn. (Source: Chris Gudgeon, *The Naked Truth*)

His cheating heart

You suspect the worst: he's having an affair. Your paranoia reaches new heights as you constantly look for signs to prove

Quickie

A typical medieval practice known as the "trial by red-hot iron" was used to test a man for infidelity. A priest blessed a red-hot iron with holy water, and the accused had to carry the iron for a distance of 9 feet. If, after being covered for 3 days, his hands were found to be festering with blood, he was deemed guilty. (Source: Richard Zacks, *History Laid Bare*)

his infidelity. No clue is too small: Why did he brush his teeth for four minutes instead of three this morning?

What do you do? Should you confront him? If you ambush him, there's a good chance he'll get on the defensive and deny it. While it's certainly your right to ask him directly, try some of the following tactics first:

- Treat your partner like gold—guilt is a powerful emotion. He may break down and confess, desperate for your forgiveness (naturally, you'll show him no mercy).
- Make references to other couples who have gone through affairs. Watch him closely for signs of discomfort, e.g., facial tics or sudden gasping for air.
- Make tonight's dinner discussion "Why people cheat" and gauge how eager he is to change the subject.
- Go to movies or read books that focus on infidelity and see if he starts to sweat.
- Trust your instincts. If you suspect foul play, make sure you have solid evidence—credit card slips, emails, phone bills, the woman's underwear you found in your bed—to back you up before you confront him.

Bedtime Story

"I was having an affair with the married woman across the street. One afternoon, as she was straddling me on her couch, I heard a key in the front door. Thankfully, I had put the chain on the door. The look on her face went from pure bliss to horror and shock. She ran to the dining room topless and hid behind a curtain. I grabbed her top and bra and threw them to her while I put my shirt on. Her husband was calling her name through the locked door. She sent me to the basement and let him in. After what seemed like an eternity, the door at the top of the stairs opened and a deep voice said, 'I think you should come up, and get out!' I grabbed my shoes by the front door and fled across the street . . . in my socks. Before I was halfway across, I heard the front door slam. Hard. Very hard."

(Jack, 30)

Now what?

Once you have confronted your partner and he has confessed to cheating on you, how should you respond?

- Indulge (briefly) in violent revenge fantasies, but do not act on them. Think of the inconvenience: as much fun as it seems like it would be to find the two of them and poke their eyes out with hot irons, where does one even find hot irons these days?
- That said, no need to get all Stepford Wife and be creepily calm and rational. You're allowed to freak out. However, avoid confrontations in the kitchen or other places where sharp objects are readily available. No need for you to end up in jail over his indiscretion.

- Don't press for details. This is painful enough. Why torture yourself?
- Decide if this is a wake-up call to deal with problems you've been avoiding in your relationship. Is the relationship worth salvaging?
- If you do decide to work it out, know that building trust after a betrayal like this is a difficult and tenuous operation. One therapist described it to me as gluing a broken china plate back together. Others may not know it's been broken, but the two of you will have a hard time forgetting.

The top five reasons people cheat

1. *The thrill.* Especially if the sex you've been having with the same person for years isn't quite the bodice-ripping flurry it once was.
2. *The distraction.* When you're not happy in your relationship, it's often easier to jump into bed with someone new than it is to work on the relationship.
3. *The ego boost.* Having someone take an interest in you when your boyfriend or husband temporarily loses sight of what a truly wonderful person you are can do wonders for your self-esteem—at least, in the short term. And doesn't your partner always like you better when you're feeling confident?
4. *The life-jolt.* It makes us feel alive. Sure, it's risky. But so is diving out of planes. And people still seem to want to do that.
5. *The mind fuck.* Infidelity helps improve your rationalization skills.

Electric sparks

Sure, there are some fuzzy lines when it comes to monogamy. For instance, which types of behaviours constitute cheating? Holding hands? Kissing? With tongue or without? Is there a cheating-free zone? That is, if you're in another city or another country and have a minor transgression, does it count? And, of course, much ink has been spilled over the most recently debated fine line in cheating: online sexual encounters. Is cybersex considered cheating? It seems pretty basic to me. You're talking dirty and whacking off with someone else. Just because you can't see the person, it doesn't absolve you of guilt. Wouldn't you feel betrayed if your boyfriend picked up some woman at a bar and brought her home, and they lay in bed and jerked off together while talking dirty? As far as I'm concerned, masturbating with someone else, whether live or over the Internet, is cheating. Of course, if you have an agreement, and you and your relationship can handle a little outside action, fine. If you can't, it has to stop.

To tell or not to tell

I once had a friend whose husband hit on me and another girlfriend of mine. This other girlfriend approached me and thought we should confront our friend and reveal to her that her husband is a lout. I wanted no part and found myself annoyed with her request. Who was I to stir up shit? Maybe she already knew the truth and had chosen to live with it. Maybe she had more tolerance than I in a relationship. Maybe she was in denial. Who knows? I didn't—and still don't—feel qualified to judge.

"But if she already knows what a jerk he is, and we reinforce it, we might be able to save her from this guy," my friend at the time insisted. "It's the sisterly thing to do."

I wasn't so sure. So I decided to solicit some advice. I asked a friend who had recently divorced a guy who had been cheating on her. "I would have liked my friends to have told me what they thought about him," she offers as an insight into my own dilemma. "But the truth is, I knew deep down what he was like but was in serious denial about it. If a friend had told me what she thought, I would probably have resented her and pushed her away. I needed to come to the realization alone."

As proof of this theory, another woman told me she lost a friend after she told her the guy she was about to marry had been unfaithful to her. "It taught me that I can't save every woman from bad men, and it is arrogant to think I can," she says. "Maybe she needs to be with him right now, even though he is a pig."

That's not to say there aren't times when you should come clean and tell a friend she is being jerked around in a relationship. It depends on your level of commitment to the friendship and what will come of telling all. Snitching on someone can be a tough call. Sometimes it's necessary, but you have to accept that you can't run you friend's life—no matter how difficult it is to see her screwed over in a relationship.

Before you spill the beans on someone you think is having an affair, ask yourself these questions:

- Why do you want to tell? Are you motivated by a sincere desire to help, or are you a drama queen who gets some kind of twisted pleasure out of stirring things up?
- Will telling the truth hurt the person needlessly? For example, if you find yourself lip-locked with a friend's boyfriend one night but you both agree it was a definite one-time mistake, telling might do more harm than good.
- How serious is the betrayal? Is it a one-time case of bad judgement or a continuing affair?
- Has your friend expressed suspicions about her partner's bad behaviour? If she already senses her partner is cheating on her and you have info that confirms it, you should probably fill her in.
- Will you be around to pick up the pieces? How close are you to the person involved, and how available will you be to deal with the fallout after the bomb drops?

What the Canuck!

According to a survey by the cable television channel Showcase, Alberta has the highest rate of cheating in Canada. Some 39% of Alberta respondents claimed to have been cheated on by a lover.

It's impolite to have sex anywhere that is visible to other people who aren't having sex.

—Jenny Éclair, author

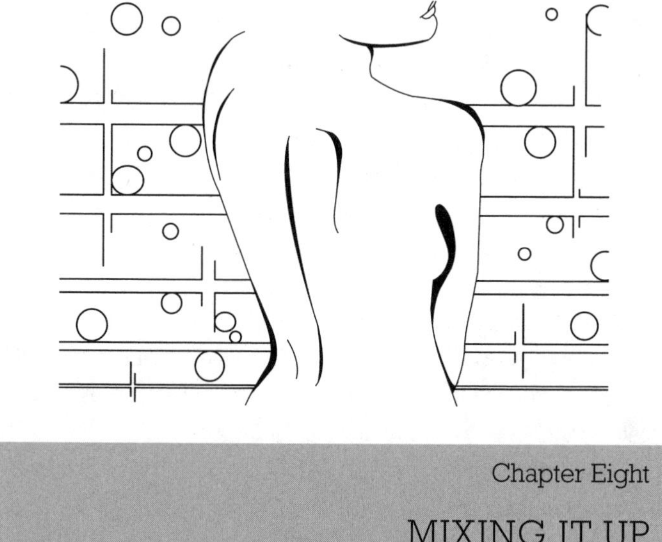

Chapter Eight

MIXING IT UP

Wash Your Mouth Out!

Talking dirty is a great way to explore fantasies and discover your limits and desires. It can also keep things interesting once you're more involved. And screaming out nasties in the heat of the moment is a great way to introduce yourself to the neighbours.

But talking dirty is a bit like talking about sex in public. Some people are comfortable with it, while others are not. Some get off on talking, the raunchier the better. Still others prefer things silent, allowing them to enjoy sex as a purely physical sensation . . . or they're just big-time shy.

Obviously our verbal skills in bed are also determined by our moods, our level of comfort with a person (or with ourselves), how horny we are and how competent any given lover is.

Here are some things to keep in mind:

- Flattery or words of encouragement are good. Just make sure you're honest. You don't want to tell him how hot his cunnilingus style is when it bores you to tears. You'll be stuck with it.
- One-night stands can be a good time to test-drive your verbal skills because there is less at stake. Mind you, if you're already shy, scoring one-night stands might be a bit of a problem.
- Don't get too analytical when talking dirty. Let's face it, sex vocabulary is limited. Stick to four-letter words.
- On the other hand, no need to regress. Baby talk is *not* hot!

Reach out and touch someone

One great way to practise talking dirty is to do it over the phone. Phone sex is an obvious way to stay intimate when you're physically separated, but it's also good practice for telling your partner what you like and for discovering his turn-ons. It usually makes things even hotter when you do finally get your grubby little hands all over each other. The biggest challenge with phone sex, however, is getting over the "I feel ridiculous" hump. Unless we've worked as phone-sex operators, most of us don't know where to begin. "What are you wearing?" gets a little tired. Well, lucky for you, I've spoken to a few phone-sex operators over the years. Here are some of their suggestions to get you going:

- Set the mood just as you would if you were together—candles, nice lighting, a glass of wine.
- Use a lot of sweet talk and a soft, low voice. Focus on each other. Tell your partner wonderful things about his body—what you like about the way it looks, the way it smells, the way it reacts to your touch.
- Use a lot of detail, which those in the professional phone-sex business emphasize is distinct from just being explicit. Describe exactly what you see happening in your mind in minute detail, and get all the senses involved.
- If your imagination isn't up to it, describe a particular hot session you've had together in the past. Describe what you liked about it.
- Use sound effects. Here's your chance to perform. Give him your best blowjob imitation, gags and all.
- If you don't want your phone-sex life to become predictable, try reading to each other from a sexy book.
- To avoid cauliflower ear and a kink in your neck, consider investing in a headset.

Quickie

Sometimes, it can be easier to write dirty than talk dirty. Emailing your smutty thoughts to your paramour is one way to virtually keep in touch when you can't be together.

Just make sure to double check the recipient's address before you hit that send button. You don't want everyone in your address book finding out all the naughty things you'd like to do to your partner.

Bedtime Story

"I once sent 'hot' letters by email to my lover's work address. Unfortunately, her boss discovered one of them and, in a very embarrassing meeting, my dearest was told how unprofessional her behaviour was and that I had to stop." **(Daniel, 31)**

Baring It All

I think most of us have fantasized about having a partner strip for us. I'd love to have a man strip for me. And I don't mean cheesy, Chippendale-style dancing, but something sexy and playful. Though the Chippendale's thing would have a certain charm if done with a sense of humour. After all, making a woman laugh is very seductive. But I'd love to see a guy in some sexy underwear, tight pants and a tight T-shirt—hell, even a garter and stockings would work if he could pull it off—just something that tells me he's put some thought into it and is 100 percent focused on me. After all, isn't that the best part of having a private dancer? Okay, it's hot to look at, but a big part of the charm is the special attention.

How do you get your partner to bare it all for you? Saying, "Hey, honey, why don't you dress up like that hottie we saw at the club the other night and strip for me," is like him saying, "Why can't you dress more like her?" Telling him in a moment of passion how much you love his body and how much of a turn-on it would be if he slowly unwrapped it for you should at least get it on his to-do list.

Doing it right

What if you want to give him a little bump and grind? Stripping for your partner is a great way to get in touch with your inner slut, something more women could stand to do. When it comes to stripping for your partner, there's really no right or wrong way. What's the big deal, after all? Slap on some music and some sexy underwear and start peeling. While there's something to be said for improvisation, if you want to really wow him, try a few of these suggestions:

- Choose your music ahead of time. Something slow and seductive is probably better than, say, metal—though, depending on who your partner is, that could work. The key is, know your audience.
- Plan your outfit ahead of time. You don't want to find yourself in clothing that is too complicated to take off.
- Set the mood. Everything looks better in candlelight.
- Take your time. There is a reason they call this a strip "tease." Accessories are good for this. Gloves, scarves and stockings all prolong the agony.
- Practise beforehand. No one's expecting a Josephine Baker–calibre performance from you, but practising a few moves in front of the mirror will not only let you know what works but will get you excited about your show.

- Keep something on, like some sexy undies or some high boots. It's always sexier to leave a little something to the imagination.
- Drop your inhibitions. Don't worry about what he thinks of your body or whether you look like an idiot. Trust me, that'll be the last thing on his mind.

Table Manners

Forget what your mom said about eating in bed; you're a grownup now, and you don't have to listen to her. Eating in bed rocks, especially if you're eating off each other's bodies. You just haven't lived until you've had a raw egg yolk sucked out of your belly button. Or been turned into a human chocolate sundae to be eaten by your partner. Good sex is all about letting yourself go. Bringing food to bed and letting things get messy is a great way to do this. If your partner's a neat freak or you're house-sitting your parents' place and don't want to muss up the sheets, consider investing in a plastic sheet (you can get plastic zip-up mattress covers from medical supply stores). And be sensitive to any food allergies your partner may have. You don't want to be explaining to the emergency room doctor why his allergy to strawberries caused such swelling down there.

Location Scouting

An easy way to perk things up in the bedroom is to get *out* of the bedroom. Just remember, there are things to consider when deciding to relocate: like the fact that public sex is illegal in Canada! Not that this seems to stop us. According to a 2004 sex poll in Toronto's *NOW* magazine, 38 percent of straight women and 51 percent of queer women enjoy public sex.

Public sex rule number 1: Be discreet. A peck on the cheek and even some brief liplocking are acceptable public displays of affection (PDA) but full-on groping on a public bus during rush hour is not. Other location-specific considerations are:

- *Sex on the beach.* If you're going to have sex on a beach, bring a blanket. It may look hot in the movies, but sand up your butt just isn't sexy. Same goes for haystacks, cement and other rough surfaces. At the very least, check on each other to make sure no one is losing too much blood.
- *Sex in public bathrooms.* Make it quick. Some people actually have to use those things to pee.
- *Sex in parks.* I know the contraptions in the playground make for some fun and interesting positions, but think of the children.
- *Sex in cars.* It's all fun and games until you get come in your eye and it blinds you and you go veering off into the ditch. Driving and sex don't mix. Just pull over. At least then all you have to endure is the embarrassment of facing the cop who suddenly comes knocking on your window.

Quickie
According to a poll commissioned by General Motors, 23% of Canadian drivers have done it in a car.

- *Sex in churches or other religious locations.* This one's between you and God.
- *Sex in the kitchen.* For your partner's safety, remove sharp objects from surfaces you'll be, um, inhabiting. Wipe down said surfaces carefully when done. Others have to eat off that table, after all.
- *Sex in the bathtub.* Be aware of your position. Having a metal faucet repeatedly rammed into your back isn't exactly a turn-on. And careful with those water jets. Shooting water into your vagina can be dangerous.
- *Sex in the shower.* Be careful not to slip, and save some hot water for the next person.

Pornography Protocol

Watch and learn

Watching porn with a lover can be a loaded proposition. Because guys grow up on the stuff and don't feel any pressure to live up to the women who are in these videos (they just get to fantasize about fucking them), they have a much less emotionally charged relationship with it. Women, on the other hand, take it very personally. Because women have spent so many years feeling objectified and offended by it, we're a little sensitive about porn. Now that we've relaxed a bit and can actually admit that sometimes, heaven forbid, we like a little visual stimuli as well, we're starting to articulate what we like and don't like in our smut. Unfortunately, because the industry has been focused for years on getting guys off, it's a little slow on the uptake in catering to female sexuality. Besides, guys are easier to cater to. Give them regular blowjobs, some penetration from every angle and a come shot and they're happy. They don't expect anything more out of porn. The industry thinks that catering to women means adding some costumes and a storyline. I'm not so sure. I think women just want to see things that get us off—hot guys, hot sex that goes beyond the usual script, and a few more women actually getting their rocks off on camera rather than faking it.

It's no wonder that, for me, watching porn with lovers in the past has more often ended in fights than in hot sex. I would get annoyed that he was getting off on images that bugged me, even while I was getting aroused by it. So now I usually just watch porn alone. That way, I can enjoy it without censoring myself because even if I'm bothered by something, I don't have to explain it to myself.

If you do decide to watch porn with a lover, it's important to be sensitive to each other's responses. If he gets excited by something that doesn't excite you, try not to hold it against him. Or try to explain why it bothers you without getting defensive. And if you see something you like, by all means, it's your chance to pipe up and let him know. It's another great way to find out what turns each other's crank. Or what doesn't.

What the Canuck!

August 2000: A young girl in Saskatoon, Saskatchewan, discovers that Wolfman bubble gum includes pornographic stick-on tattoos depicting women in bondage.

Tantric Tips

As I've been saying all along, good sexual etiquette boils down to having respect and consideration for your partner. This is old news for Tantric sex practitioners, who, more than 5,000 years ago, made this ancient sexual art popular in India and Tibet.

Tantric sex combines breathing, chanting and sexual yoga to achieve spiritual enlightenment and rock your sex life. Part of the practice involves the nifty trick of him learning how to come without spurting, as ejaculation is believed to deplete a man's spiritual and life energy. He'll also dig it because his orgasm will feel more like the full-body orgasm he enviously sees us ladies enjoying so much.

There are plenty of books and web resources that will help you learn how to practise Tantric sex. In the meantime, here are some ideas for how to bring up the subject in the first place:

- Wrap up a Tantric sex book in beautiful fabric and give it to your partner.
- Make his next birthday gift a trip to a Tantra sex weekend like the ones hosted by Al Link and Pala Copeland (www.tantra-sex.com).
- Start simple. Set aside a ten-minute block each day to focus on each other without sex as a goal.
- Focus on breathing together, and following the rhythm of each other's breath.
- Give him a sensual massage without having it lead to sex.
- Set the mood by dressing up your space with candles, nice fabrics and yummy smelling oils.

- Part of Tantric tradition is to create rituals to help focus the mind on each other. Gifts of flowers, food and wine before sexual ceremonies are encouraged.

As I said, Tantric sex is all about mutual respect and support. Here are a few other things to keep in mind while staring into each other's third eye.

- Don't be judgmental. There is no "right" way to do this.
- No pressure. Don't expect a seven-hour orgasm the first time out.
- Let yourself feel silly. Laughing together is sexy.

Such a chakra

The ancient Eastern tradition of Tantra teaches that sex involves the mind and the spirit as well as the body. The idea is to think of sex beyond orgasm and as a way of achieving a higher state of consciousness. Central to Tantric sexual practices are the chakras, seven major energy centres throughout the body that are stimulated in different ways:

Ajna—Also referred to as "the third eye." Located between the eyebrows and associated with higher knowledge, intellect and compassion.

Anahat—Known as the heart chakra and located between the nipples. It's associated with love, empathy, joy and the union of body and spirit, as well as the merging of male and female polar energies.

What the Canuck!

In Quebec, as late as 1959, *Lady Chatterly's Lover* was considered criminally obscene. (Source: Jeffrey Miller, *Ardor in the Court!*)

Quickie

In Taoist sexual tradition, much emphasis is placed on different types of penile thrusting during intercourse. A sequence of 9 shallow thrusts followed by a single deep one is especially favoured, partly because 9 is considered a magical number. (Source: Sarah Dening, *The Mythology of Sex*)

Manipur—Located on the solar plexus and associated with intellect, power, will, ego and action.

Muladhara—Located at the base of the sex organs and associated with survival and sexuality, pain and pleasure.

Sahasrara—Located above the crown of the head and associated with self-realization, cosmic consciousness, bliss and total unity with the whole.

Swadhishtana—Located just below the navel, and the source of vital life energy. It relates to emotion, reproduction and sexual drive.

Vishuddha—Located in the throat and associated with self-awareness, purity, expression and communication.

If it happens that you do want peanut butter in bed while you're having sex and your partner doesn't, in the long run the thing to do may be to find another partner.

—**Dr. Ruth Westheimer, psychologist and sex educator**

Chapter Nine

THINK KINK

Fantasy Forward

While it's probably a little presumptuous to expect him to pee in your mouth on a first date, at what point do you reveal to a partner that you might be up for something a little kinky? Certainly, the longer you're with someone, the deeper into routine you fall and the tougher it becomes to tell your partner you'd like to push your sexual limits. What if you reveal something you'd like to try and your partner thinks you're a freak or a pervert and leaves you? Yes, sharing fantasies is delicate work requiring tact and sensitivity. Try these tips:

- Find an appropriate time to reveal fantasies. I find that long car rides are good for this, as are walks in the park, on the beach, in the country—any neutral, relaxed environment that allows you to ask questions, swap fantasies and reveal inhibitions without fearing you'll be laughed out of bed. It's best to be somewhere quasi-private as well, in case you suddenly feel inspired to act out the discussion. Unless, of course, public sex is one of your fantasies.
- It's extremely ill-mannered to try to force a sexual fantasy on a partner. After all, sexual compatibility is not always guaranteed, especially when you get into some of the more fancy stuff. All you can do is try to accept this, and—if your partner's particular kink doesn't make you want to hurl—indulge him once in a while and hope he will return the favour.
- When venturing into new territory and taking a lover with you, respect is paramount. If you absolutely can't handle his sexual kinks, he has to respect that and decide if he can live without them.
- Communication is essential. Check in regularly to make sure you're both okay physically and emotionally, and take things slow, stopping whenever either of you feels uncomfortable or ridiculous.
- Realize that reality sometimes doesn't live up to fantasy. Wearing diapers and being treated like a baby might

have seemed like a turn-on in your mind, but you might find yourself less than gaga about the real thing. The thought of being in a threesome may excite you, but the reality of it might be threatening, or might make you feel silly or scared.

- Be careful. It's all fun and games until someone's penis gets stuck in a body bag, that nifty zip-up leather bodysuit you thought would be fun to play "sensory deprivation" with (yes, this happened to someone I know).
- Lest you think the only way to introduce kinky sex into your life is to don a leather hood or lead your honey around on a collar and chain, I assure you that even "vanilla" couples can experiment without buying into a lifestyle. For many people, tying a lover's hands to the bed with a scarf is as far as they're going to go, and that's just fine. (Not always the best restraint BTW. See Fit to Be Tied on page 141 for more info on playing with bondage.)
- Rediscover your inner child. Sexual experimentation should be fun. Remember how to play. Testing new waters with a lover can be exhilarating, hilarious and completely hot. It's a wonderful way to increase intimacy. It can also be terrifying. Which is why so many of us never get around to it. But, as the old saying goes, "Nothing like a nice golden shower to bring two people together."
- If you're intimidated by new things, start with something really simple like a blindfold. By taking away one sense, you'll feel the others more acutely. A blindfold also allows you to play with power, as one partner has the benefit of

sight. If you get freaked, all you have to do is push the blindfold up.

- There are certain fantasies you probably shouldn't reveal to anyone but your psychiatrist, such as those involving family members, children, dead people or animals. I'd also suggest you avoid revealing fantasies that involve anyone hotter than your partner, especially if he's your partner's best friend.

Dominatrix Lady Green, author of *The Sexually Dominant Woman*, suggests a "yes/no/maybe" exercise for couples who want to expand their sexual horizons. Write down every sexual activity you've heard of, whether it sounds fun or gross or whatever. Don't censor yourselves. Then, using different coloured pens, mark a Y, N or M beside each item on the list to indicate your comfort level with that activity. Now you've got a game plan. Those activities that got a "yes" from both of you are a go, those that got a "maybe" from either of you get discussed and those that got a "no" from either of you get crossed off the list.

Disciplinary Action

Spanking can be fun, whether you're into some light bum paddling or a full-on whumping. There are lots of lovely nerve endings in your bum, and pain releases endorphins that make you feel all goofy and light-headed. Then there's the psychological pleasure in disciplining someone because he's been "naughty," not to mention the whole head-trip of submission and domination or control. However, there are several physical and psychological aspects of spanking that need to be considered before you go in swinging.

Do

- Ease him into it by telling him exactly what you're doing every step of the way.
- Warm things up with a little bum massage and some pinching and squeezing. This prepares the bum for what's to come and causes the brain to release neurotransmitters that up the pain threshold.
- Manage expectations. The perfect spanking you have in mind might not play out in reality. You might feel silly, embarrassed or even turned off. This is normal.
- Make sure you can trust your partner to respect your limits and that you are with someone with whom you are able to communicate your needs.
- Know your instrument. If you're using an implement to whoop your partner, know that hard, flat surfaces—like paddles—can bruise, while whips and crops sting. Make sure you know how to operate the machinery.
- Breathe. Conscious breathing and relaxation techniques can help the pain flow through you.
- Stay alert. You don't want to be drifting off while someone's caning your bare ass.
- Have a safe-word so you know when the play needs to stop.
- Do your homework. If you're going to get into serious corporal stuff, there are plenty of resources online and in

books. (Try Lady Green's *The Compleat Spanker*, for example, or go online to www.sexuality.org/l/bdsm/sss-faq.html for all your spanking inquiries.)

Don't

- Haul off in the middle of sex and start giving your honey a good ass-slapping. Sure, sometimes things get hot and heavy and before you know it someone's getting their ass smacked, but a more considerate approach would be to talk about it first. Your partner might have psychological boundaries when it comes to physical pain or might simply not be into it.
- Push it if your partner isn't into it.
- Smack your honey near the tailbone and lower back: that's where the kidneys are, and he won't like it. Keep action on the fleshy bits of the bum cheeks.
- Get into heavy spanking if you've been drinking or doing mind-altering drugs.

When it comes to heavy kinky play involving bondage and discipline, dominance and submission, sadism and masochism (BDSM), there is one strict rule: first drink of the day ends the play. Same goes for drugs. An experienced bondage practitioner explains that while sensory deprivation is the goal, you need your senses to be in proper working order before you can deprive them.

Mistress, may I?

Here are some of the more common BDSM terms so you can wow 'em the next time you're down at the fetish club:

BDSM—It is generally accepted within the scene that these initials stand for bondage and domination, domination and submission, and sadism and masochism.

Body modification—To have the body modified by piercing or cutting.

Bottom—Another term for a submissive.

Caning—Beating with a cane, usually on the buttocks, often done in school-scene games.

CBT—Cock-and-ball torture, i.e., playing with, restraining, tying, lightly slapping or pinching his genitals.

Dom—A male dominant.

Domina, Domme, Dominant, Dominatrix—Various terms that may be used to describe a Mistress.

Dungeon—Most Mistresses refer to the room where they play as a dungeon. Some dungeons are decorated and equipped in the style of medieval torture chambers, but the term covers any room equipped for BDSM. Can also be referred to as a chamber.

Edge-play—This means that the scene will be taken to extreme limits. Danger to health is implied, such as with blood sports, cutting and electrical stimulation. Only those experienced in BDSM should contemplate edge-play—it is definitely not for the novice.

Medical scenes—Scenes in which the Mistress plays the role of doctor or nurse. They often involve rectal exams, enemas and catheters. Occasionally, body-neutral fluids are injected under the skin.

Pet training—To be trained as a dog, pony or other pet.

Safe-word—Any Mistress worth her salt will give you a safe-word before you start playing. Use of the word instantly stops play. It is used when your limits have been reached. Never play without a safe-word.

S.S.C.—Safe, Sane, Consensual. What all BDSM play or scenes should be.

Switch—Someone who goes back and forth between being a top and a bottom.

Top—Another term for a dominant.

Vanilla—Descriptive of people who are not active in the BDSM scene.

Bedtime Story

"My Mistress decided she and a friend were going to take me out for dinner. When we sat down at the restaurant, Mistress noticed that I sat on the back of my skirt (a big no-no for her). She grabbed me by my hand, asked her friend to hold the booth and escorted me out to the car, where she bent me over the hood, lifted my skirt up and, taking a strap, gave me fifty stripes on my bum. I had to bite my lip to keep from screaming. She escorted me back to our table, and this time I raised my skirt so I would not sit on it. The vinyl seat was torture on my freshly whipped bum. I noticed I was getting strange looks from other people in the restaurant. I later found out that Mistress's friend was watching my whipping from the window of the restaurant, and several customers walked up to see what she was looking at and chuckling about. My private punishment session turned out to be a lot more public than I thought. Needless to say, I never made that mistake again." **(Kelly, 33)**

Fit to Be Tied

If you've ever held your lover's wrists while having sex, you've practised bondage. It's not exactly erotic Japanese rope bondage (Fetish Diva Midori's site, beautybound.com, has some amazing examples of this), but you're still playing with the idea of restraining your partner. Using restraints can be a wonderful way to play with power and sensory deprivation, and to develop trust with a partner. But trust goes hand in hand with respect, and if you're going to play with bondage you have to follow proper procedure. After all, you don't want to be hooded and gagged and suddenly hear your partner rummaging through the knife drawer in the kitchen.

Do

- Introduce bondage with care. Roping your honey like a rodeo calf the first time out isn't very polite. Start slow.

Try simply holding his wrists and see how he responds to that before hauling out the full leather and chains.

- Test your powers of domination and control. Tell him to hold his hands behind his back and not to move them until you tell him to. See how well he listens.
- Use cotton ropes when getting into more serious bondage. They are the most comfortable and wash up easily.
- Make sure your partner is comfortable. I know you want him to feel restrained, but he doesn't need to be in pain.
- Make sure you can get him out of the bonds easily if necessary, say if he suddenly passes out. It's a good idea to keep a pair of scissors handy for just such an occasion.
- Let him go pee before you tie him up, unless you both agree to incorporate that into your play.

Don't

- Tie someone spread-eagle on the bed. This is often the first thing people do when tying up a partner. But stretching out someone's arms for an extended period of time can actually interfere with his breathing. The joke in bondage circles is that Jesus died from asphyxiation, not from hanging there.
- Use scarves. Sure they're pretty, and most of us have them lying around the house, but the knots get tighter as you pull on them and can be hard to undo.
- Use cheap handcuffs. They make lousy restraints, as the metal cuts into your skin and most don't have the mechanism to stop them from tightening around the wrist. That's no way to treat a lover, now is it?

- Use nylon rope. It tends to slip.
- Keep anyone tied up for more than twenty minutes, just in case you're cutting off circulation.

Toy Story

Sex toys are another wonderfully simple way to spice things up. But how do you incorporate them without freaking out your partner or making him feel like he's being replaced? Certainly not by hauling in a three-foot dildo and saying, "Honey, look what I've got! Mind if I shove it up your bum?" Ease your way into sex-toy territory with some of the following tips:

- Start small and quiet.
- At least try to make it look like you want him involved. Let him run the controls while you operate the machinery.
- Go sex-toy shopping together. You no longer have to wear a trench coat to visit your local sex store. Most larger cities in Canada have sex shops that are couple- and female-friendly, with informed and open-minded staff members who make it easy to ask even the most delicate questions.
- Be sensitive to your partner's level of comfort in a sex shop. Not everyone feels at home when faced with a wall of Hot Rods, Clit Kissers, Dragon Ladies and Mini-Pearls. Make your first time out an exploratory mission with no pressure to buy anything. Stick close to your partner and pay attention to what draws his attention.

- When choosing toys, consider how powerful a toy you need. Women who can come from manual stimulation or are easily orgasmic will be fine with a model that takes two AA batteries. If orgasm is more difficult for you, you might consider something stronger, or even a plug-in. If you want a good buzz and don't necessarily want penetration, egg-shaped vibrators, sometimes called Silver Bullets or Mini-Pearls, are great.
- Rule out anything you don't like. Personally, I'm not a big fan of toys that look like real sex organs. They creep me out.
- Don't make the mistake a lot of guys make: just because they want to have a really big dick doesn't mean you do.
- If you've never tried a sex toy, start out with something inexpensive—$20 to $30—to see if you like it before you shell out big bucks for something more durable.

Toy talk

When it comes to sex toys, there's a lot of crap out there. Before you waste your money, do your research. This will get you started:

Anal beads—Resembling a string of pearls (but made out of plastic, rubber, silicone or jelly rubber), anal beads are inserted into the anus one at a time. Pleasurable sensation is provided when the bead is popped into or pulled out of the anus, often at the point of orgasm.

Ben-wa balls—Small metal balls (three-quarters to one inch in diameter that are inserted into the vagina. Ben-wa balls produce sensations when they rub against the inside of the vagina or when they knock up against each other.

Butt plug—A sex toy with a flared base (so it won't get lost in your bum) that is inserted into the anus and left in while the wearer engages in other types of play and stimulation.

Cock ring—A ring made of metal, rubber or leather worn around the base of the penis to control blood flow. A cock ring can help sustain an erection, or can prevent one if applied to a flaccid penis.

Dildo—A non-vibrating phallic-shaped sex toy used for oral, anal and vaginal penetration; available in various styles, sizes and materials.

Dong—Another word for dildo; "dong" commonly refers to penis-shaped dildos, which are often moulded from a man's penis and designed with veins and testicles.

Double-ended—A long dildo (twelve to eighteen inches in length) with a head on each end. Allows two partners to penetrate each other at the same time or simultaneous vaginal and anal penetration on one person.

Strap-on—A dildo, usually with a flared base, that can be secured into a harness.

Vibrator—Any toy with a motor that vibrates; can be battery-operated, plug-in (electric) or battery-rechargeable, and, depending on the type, used for internal or external use.

Types of vibrators

Battery-operated—Available in a wide variety of styles and materials, these are generally not as strong as the electric vibrators, but unlike electric vibes, some have a dual purpose: vaginal penetration and clitoral stimulation at once. Bonus—you can walk around the house while using it.

Coil-operated—Vibrators that are run by an electromagnetic coil rather than a motor. Quieter and lighter, these provide more intense vibrations. Most come with attachments.

G-spot—A curved vibrator intended to stimulate the G-spot when inserted. Firm or hard materials are preferred so the vibe doesn't bend or flex once inserted into the vagina.

Mini massagers—Tiny battery-operated sex toys (like the Pocket Rocket or Fukuoku 9000) that provide powerful clitoral stimulation. For external genital stimulation only.

Multi-purpose—Vibes with a long shaft for penetration as well as an extra clitoral vibrator at the base, with separate controls for both parts. The now-famous Rabbit Pearl used on *Sex and the City* fits into this category.

Plug-in—Electric vibrators that provide stronger sensations; usually used for external genital stimulation, although attachments are available for anal and vaginal penetration. Some (like the Hitachi Magic Wand, often referred to as the Cadillac of Vibrators) have a cup-like attachment for penile stimulation. They never let you down at that crucial moment as battery-operated vibes can.

Vibrating egg/bullet—Egg-shaped vibes made out of hard plastic and sometimes covered in soft vinyl or rubber. Attached to an external battery pack with controls. Cheap, effective and usually quiet, they are small enough to cup in your hand to stimulate the clitoris during intercourse. They can also can be strapped into a harness for hands-free clitoral stimulation.

Waterproof—Battery-operated sex toys covered in special water-resistant materials for water play.

Sex toy materials

Cyberskin—Sex toys made with this material simulate the softness of real human skin (or tissue, like vaginal lips) and the rigidity of erectile tissue; cyberskin is extremely realistic, flexible and highly resilient.

Jelly—A pliable but reasonably firm material, jelly quickly warms up to body temperature upon penetration. Jelly is porous, making it more difficult to clean, so using condoms over jelly toys is recommended. Don't leave them lying under your bed with the dust bunnies. Gross.

Plastic—Sex toys made from plastic are hard and cold, but are very smooth for insertion; these are usually the cheapest kind to purchase, but tend to be poor in quality.

Silicone—A synthetic material that is ideal for sex toys, as it is soft and smooth, hypoallergenic, non-porous (making it easy to clean) and durable. It also retains body heat. Slightly more expensive, but worth it.

It seems that most people can more comfortably discuss murder and rape than anal pleasure.

—Jack Morin, author of Anal Pleasure and Health

The Bottom Line

A friend of mine told me about a guy she slept with who decided he wanted to have anal sex. They were doing it doggie style, and he suddenly yelled, "Heads up!" and tried to stick his penis into her bum. Needless to say, this is the perfect example of how *not* to introduce the idea of anal sex.

Bum sex is a delicate topic many of us don't want to talk about, never mind try. We've been taught that our butts are private and dirty, and a one-way street. Then there are all the myths flying around about people getting things lost in their butts, or losing bowel control or hurting themselves and ending up in hospital. It's enough to make anyone's sphincter tighten up.

But, as Jack Morin writes in his book *Anal Pleasure & Health*, "taboos . . . don't necessarily eliminate the impulses and behaviors they forbid. Instead, these desires go 'underground,' both individually and collectively . . . In this way, a taboo gives the forbidden feeling or behavior an inflated significance." As is evidenced by the glut of rectally inspired porn flicks: *Anal Angel*, *Hot Tales from the Backside*, *Analmania*, *Rearing Rachel*, *Anal Security Squad*, *Backing In*, *Backdoor Brides* . . . the list goes on. And since men are still the primary consumers of porn, next thing you know they're knocking at your back door, trying to persuade you to "*Try* it—you'll like it."

Only you're thinking, "Ick. Nice girls don't do that." Or if they do, it's only to please their male partner, right? Not true and not true. Done right, anal sex can be incredibly intense, pleasurable and intimate, and believe or not, some women actually like it! The combination of the trust it creates between the two of you, the fact that it is a still a little taboo (there is an upside to having things be naughty) and the fact that the bum is full of wonderful nerves and sensations can make anal sex very hot.

Part of the problem is that porn movies make it look like you can go from zero to sixty without any warm-up: guys start shoving and you're left screaming. Then guys wonder why their female partner isn't into anal sex. Guess what? Porn is edited to look like that. Even the pros need a little warm-up.

If you're going to try bum sex, be polite and do it right:

- Relax and take it *slow*.
- Use lots and lots (and lots) of lube.
- You set the pace and control the action.
- Draw his penis (or your phallic object of choice) in as your sphincter relaxes instead of having him push his way in.
- Don't forget the condom. Bum tissue tears easily—very HIV-friendly.
- It's okay to go from vaginal intercourse to anal intercourse, but don't let him go back to vaginal intercourse after he has penetrated you anally without changing the condom. You'll transfer bacteria from the anus to the vagina, and your vagina won't be happy about it.

Quickie

Fudge-packing, browning, corking, playing mud darts, whatever you call it, anal sex is still illegal in several southern and Midwestern states—though in Texas it's okay as long as you're not gay (of course, having sex with, or even marrying, your first cousin is just fine).

I have a little bit of penis envy. Yeah, they're ridiculous, but they're cool.

—kd lang, singer

Fun for boys too!

Why should girls and gay men get to have all the fun? Straight boys can enjoy bum sex too. In fact, the male prostate—some equate it to the female G-spot—is just along the upper inside wall of his posterior and a finger (or dildo) up his bum right at the point of orgasm can really kick things up a notch.

It's a pleasure more men would like to explore, but many of us still get weirded out by it, thinking a straight guy who likes it up the bum must be a closet case or that it's gross or perverted. Plus, we're so locked into the idea that girls are entered and boys do the entering that we have a hard time switching roles. It's wonderful to mess with that dynamic—that is, for a guy to discover what it's like to be penetrated and for a woman to do the penetrating. But how do you bring it up?

- Choose a time when you're both relaxed and feeling open to new things.
- Mention that you've been reading about strap-on dildos recently and are intrigued by the idea of fucking him.
- Look at sex-toy catalogues together and decide on something you both might like. A word of advice: I know boys are often obsessed with size, but trust me, in this case, you'd best start small. Remind him that you are going to be—gently—ramming this thing up his butt.
- Rent a porn movie that features strap-on play and see how it works for both of you.
- Once you get him on-side and you get yourself a dildo model you like, you're in.

- As for actually doing it, three bits of advice: take it slow, lube and lube some more.

Siderodromophilia and Other Sexual Practices They Didn't Teach You in School

For every object, practice or human behaviour that exists out there, there's someone who has found a way to sexualize it and give it a funky name. Here are just a few terms to expand your unusual sexual practice repertoire. Now you'll know what to call it the next time your partner wears diapers to bed . . .

Accousticophilia—Sexual arousal by sounds.

Acrotomophilia—Arousal at the thought of having sex with an amputee.

Agalmatophilia—A mannequin or statue fetish.

Autoerotic asphyxia—Self-induced strangling or suffocation during masturbation.

Chubby chasers—Nickname for someone who is sexually aroused by an obese partner.

Coprophilia—Sexual arousal from excrement.

Feeders—People who are sexually aroused by watching their partner eat and become obese.

Fisting—Inserting a hand or fist into the anus or vagina.

Gainers—People who are sexually aroused by gaining weight.

Infantalism—Arousal from playing the role of a baby.

Quickie

According to bestiality laws of 1400 BC, "If a man does evil with a head of cattle, it is a capital crime and he shall be killed. If a man does evil with a sheep, it is a capital crime and he shall be killed. If anyone does evil with a pig, he shall die. If a man does evil with a horse or mule, there shall be no punishment." (Source: Richard Zacks, *History Laid Bare*)

Kleptophilia—Sexual arousal from stealing.

Necrophilia—An erotic attraction to corpses.

Nymphomania—Term used for women who have an insatiable appetite for sex.

Paraphilia—Unlike fetishism, in which a person is aroused by a particular object or activity, paraphilia is a condition whereby a man or a woman is completely dependent on a particular object or activity to become sexually aroused; that is, they can not become aroused without it. For example, while a foot fetishist might enjoy foot play on occasion, a paraphilic would not be able to become aroused by anything other than feet.

Podophilia—Sexual arousal by feet.

Pyrophilia—Sexual arousal by fire.

Satyriasis—The male equivalent of nymphomania.

Scopophilia—More commonly referred to as exhibitionism; arousal from exposing genitalia in taboo places.

Siderodromophilia—Arousal by trains.

Trichophilia—Any kind of hair fetish.

Water sports—Using urine in sex play.

Zoophilia—Sexual arousal by animals.

I believe that sex is a beautiful thing between two people. Between five, it's fantastic.

—Woody Allen,
filmmaker

Chapter Ten

THE MORE THE MERRIER

Three's a Crowd?

It's one thing to figure out the best way to introduce a new sex toy to your partner—if he doesn't like it, you can just toss the thing aside and get back to what you were doing—but introducing a third person into sex is a little more complicated. You can't just pull another guy out of your bag and say, "Look what I brought home, honey!"

Bringing in a third party requires tact, careful consideration and a huge amount of trust and respect for your partner. First of all, you have to gingerly explore whether your sweetie is into sharing. This can be delicate because initiating a threesome can trigger all kinds of reactions. He might feel that you think he's inadequate, or that you're unhappy with your sex life and subsequently with the relationship. Or he may jump for joy and shout, "Oh, honey, I thought you'd never ask!"

Try bringing it up in a way that is flattering to your partner, like telling him how hot you think it would be to see him with someone else. You can also simply ask for it as a favour, or maybe as a birthday present.

If he's not into it, don't accuse him of being uptight or closed-minded. You'll just piss him off and lessen your chances of it ever happening. Gently find out why he's reluctant and try to have an open-minded discussion about it. Maybe he'll come around. No pressure, though.

If you decide you're both game, there are several things to consider:

- Do you want to be with another man or another woman? Most guys don't count on this question because they've spent their whole lives looking at porn in which a threesome is always two women and a guy.
- The theory is very different from the reality. There are plenty of stories of men eager to try a threesome and a girlfriend who was less enthusiastic, but when they actually got into it, he freaked out and she loved it.
- The reality of seeing your partner getting it on with someone other than yourself can be more than you bargained for.
- It's often a good idea to find a third party who is a stranger

to both of you (the best way to do this is to take out a classified ad and screen applicants) rather than risk messing with an existing friendship.

- Before trying this in real life, watch some porn with threesome scenes together to see how that sits with both of you.
- Go to a strip club together (male or female) and buy your partner a lap dance. If uncomfortable stuff comes up for either of you, you can get up and leave and the dancer won't care.
- Try threesome phone sex first and see how that makes you feel.

The key to making a threesome work is, as with most things sexual, communication. Feelings of jealousy and insecurity may still take you by surprise, but at least if you've talked about it beforehand, you are more psychologically prepared.

It's a good idea to lay down some ground rules before you engage in a threesome. For example:

- Establish a verbal or physical signal with your partner that you can use if either of you wants to stop at any point in the action. This beats slamming the door and walking out.
- Watch for and respect this signal . . . even if you're really into it.
- Pay attention to how much time you spend on any one member of the threesome. One of the common problems that comes up in threesomes is that two people really get into each other and the third person feels left out.

Quickie

Advice to monks, circa AD 370: "When sharing 3 to a bed, always have an old man sleep in the middle." (Source: Richard Zacks, *History Laid Bare*)

- Respect each other at all times. This will help you avoid criticizing each other's behaviour or saying mean things to each other in front of the third party out of jealousy or hurt.

Group Behaviour

I can't imagine people at an orgy back in Greco-Roman times sitting around in a circle in their togas discussing their boundaries. And while the dictionary defines orgy as "wild, drunken or licentious festivity or revelry," most people I've spoken to who organize sex parties don't allow booze at their events. There's too much risk of losing control of the situation, they tell me. Besides, booze and drugs blur lines of consent, which is a big concern when you have a bunch of adults who barely know each other in a room having sex.

Kristine M, who has organized sex parties in Toronto, says she finds other ways to break the ice, such as handing everyone in the room a piece of paper and asking them to write down three sexual activities they would enjoy. She sticks the pieces of paper in a hat, and has everyone pick one and read it out: "Someone in the room likes having their toes licked."

This helps set the tone, overcomes embarrassment about telling people what you like and sparks ideas, she tells me. "And the really fun part is that over the course of the evening, you can try to find the person who matches the list you picked," says Ms. M.

Other than finding out who likes having their toes sucked, however, the logistics of organizing a sex party are much the same as organizing any kind of group gathering. You need guests, and you need a venue, a scene and music.

Ms. M offers a few other guidelines to help facilitate a successful orgy:

- Determine the sexual orientation of the group: heterosexual, homosexual or bisexual. Is it mixed co-ed?
- Learn people's parameters and what they are looking for. A go-around usually takes care of this. "Hi, I'm so-and-so, and I like girls, but I'm willing to experiment with boys, and I like oral sex, nipple tweaking and soft nibbles behind my knees."
- Invite a few people who are willing to get things started. People are usually nervous about making the first move. You need one or two people who will act as catalysts and inspire the others.
- Always invite twice as many women as men because only half the women are going to show up.
- Screen couples separately. Guys will convince their girlfriends to come when they don't really want to.
- Whether you decide to hold the orgy in someone's home or in a hotel room where everyone kicks in for the cost, it's a good idea to designate a chill-out no-sex space where people can retreat if they get stressed or freaked out.
- A theme is good, especially if you have a lot of first-timers. You might want to go with an exotic, cheesy harem theme complete with Middle Eastern music and meat pies. Or you could go Japanese red-light district and serve sushi.

Quickie

The Etruscans loved to drink and have sex. After they had finished drinking and were ready for bed, the servants would bring them courtesans, beautiful boys or their wives. Once the husbands had enjoyed any of these, the servants would then fetch lusty young men who would also fool around with these courtesans, boys or wives. (Source: Richard Zacks, *History Laid Bare*)

- Food and drink are very important. Fruits like grapes and strawberries are good. Protein is also important. Sex is a lot of work.
- Advise your guests not to go sticking anything into anyone without covering it up first. Condoms are a must.
- Tell your guests that no means no. If someone declines advances or wants to stop something that's already started, his or her wishes must be respected.
- And finally, after you leave the orgy, remember your manners. If you run into an orgy mate on the street and your unsuspecting friend asks how the two of you met, practise good etiquette and don't shout out, "Oh, we met at the orgy."

In the Swing

Maybe I just don't have the guts to be a swinger. Call me crazy, but I think I'd get a little testy watching my boyfriend get it on with another woman. Besides, I don't own a pantsuit. It sounds so seventies, doesn't it? Swinging, partner swapping, Roman sex—whatever you call it, it also sounds like asking for trouble. It'd be like deciding to stick to one flavour of ice cream and then hanging out at Ben & Jerry's. What if I tried another flavour and decided I like it better? Sure, honey, you go off and have sex with the chick with the gorgeous breasts, I'll see if I can't find a nice boy who turns my crank." I can't quite wrap my mind around it. But there are many who disagree: an estimated million swingers in Canada alone.

"I did not want to have another relationship or fall in love with someone else," a female swinger from Montreal told me. "However, I had only had sex with one other person before meeting my boyfriend. I was intrigued with the idea of having sex with other people, with different bodies and their different personalities. I wanted to see him with other people and have him watch me with others. I was also attracted to other women and wanted to explore my bisexuality."

"There's a great freedom when you're in the mattress room, naked, lights low and everyone is grabbing, touching, licking. It's a liberating experience, especially for women," says Dr. Steve Mason, a fifty-plus happily married swinger (who doesn't actively swing these days) from California. Mason, a spokesperson for the 35,000-member North American Lifestyles Organization (and who, incidentally, was the centrefold for *Playgirl*'s twentieth-anniversary issue), says that men are usually the ones who convince their women to go, but adds that more often than not the women get into it because they find it empowering to be allowed to be blatantly sexual. "Women tell me over and over that it makes them feel in charge and in control."

Swinging's not for everyone, as the folks on the Swinging Lifestyle (swingerslifestyle.net) website fully admit. But for couples that enjoy it and do it right, "a good relationship can blossom" between them. A bad relationship—which will sour anyway, they say—will definitely become more problematic.

Quickie

Between 15% and 25% of all American married couples will engage in swinging at some point in their marriage. A study of swinging couples reported greater intimacy between the partners and a decrease in sexist expectations. (Source: North American Swing Club Association)

But swinging is not the big, free, all-you-can-eat smorgasbord of human flesh most people imagine. There is plenty of etiquette to be observed when it comes to living "the Lifestyle":

- Most swingers won't have sex with anyone whose partner doesn't know he or she is sleeping with other people.
- Make rules with each other ahead of time about your limits. You might both agree anal sex is off limits, for example.
- You must be prepared to stop as soon as one of you feels uncomfortable.
- Condoms are a must.
- You must be courteous, respectful and friendly. Never be pushy. Mutual consent is rule #1, and no means no.
- You must learn to say no without hurting feelings. (The trick: no explanations; just a simple "No, thank you" will save you from trying to explain that you find him butt ugly.)
- Don't use swinging as a way to heal a bad relationship.

Swinging lingo

Along with the strict etiquette involved in swinging, there are some terms you'll definitely need to know:

"The Lifestyle"—Another term for the swinging scene.
Soft swing—No intercourse is involved.
Full swap—Intercourse is involved.

Open swinging—Having sex in the same room and/or bed with your primary partner and another couple.

Closed swinging—Being with another partner in a separate room away from your primary partner.

If you want to get "into the swing" through the personal ads, you'll want to know how to read them first:

Term	**Meaning**
Bi/Bi-sexual	Enjoys sex with either men or women
D&D free	Drug and disease free
IR couple	Interracial couple
MWC	Married white couple
Playing	Polite way of saying "having sex"
SO	Significant other/spouse
Str8/Straight	Heterosexual (sex with opposite sex only)
SWM/F	Single white male/female

Polyamory Propriety

A relatively new word, "polyamory" is an umbrella term used to describe the practice of being involved in or open to multiple loving relationships. Some people have a primary relationship to which they are emotionally monogamous but physically non-monogamous—meaning they can have sex with others, but can't fall in love, for example.

I once tried to maintain a relationship with two guys at the same time. Each sort of knew about it, but, I'll admit, I wasn't

What the Canuck!

July 2003: Municipal Court judge Denis Boisvert rules that Club L'Orage, a swingers club in Montreal, is a "common bawdy house" since the club advertises to the public. Quebec's swingers interpret the ruling as legalizing group sex as long as it is in a non-public place. (Source: *Toronto Star*)

entirely honest with either of them about the extent of the relationship with the other guy. I loved it. My ego, along with another delicate part of me, was getting constant stroking. I felt quite clever and mature. I figured, why limit my love to one guy? There's lots of me to go around, and neither of these guys had everything I wanted in a partner. Together, however, they covered a lot of ground. Things were going swimmingly, I thought, until I collapsed from sheer mental and physical exhaustion. And they tired of sharing. The first guy got out; the second stuck around so we could drag out a going-nowhere relationship for a while longer.

So it is with some admiration and, yes, some trepidation that I have approached the few polyamorists I have met over the years. One thirty-five-year-old woman I'll call Linda, who usually has a couple of relationships on the go plus some extra booty on the side, explained its appeal to me like this: "What I like about polyamory is that because you have to make your own rules, you have to be clear and overtly negotiate everything. You have to be on top of your own shit . . . No one sits and thinks, 'Okay, how do I be heterosexual and monogamous?' There is an unwritten rulebook that we all implicitly follow."

The whole point of polyamory is to make your own rules when it comes to negotiating your relationships, making it difficult to follow specific etiquette. However, mutual respect and, yes, staying on top of your own shit are necessary general guidelines to follow. Otherwise, the rules vary according to your personal needs, your morals, the needs and expectations of the other individuals involved and how much free time you have on your hands. Consider, for example, Linda's "Rules of Polyamory":

- When seeing two people, she guarantees them only a limited amount of time within a two-week period. She may see them more than that, but they can't demand it.
- She negotiates no-date nights. If it's a no-date night and they're all in the same space, she won't go home with either of them.
- If she gets involved with someone and it looks like it might get serious, she won't get involved with anyone else until at least ten months into the first relationship, once she's laid some groundwork.
- Not surprisingly, she requires all her lovers to have therapists.
- She takes at least three months after ending a relationship to process what she's learned before starting something new.

Sounds like a lot of work. Which is probably why so many people would rather fall blindly into monogamy and just cheat on each other instead.

Alternative arrangements

If you thought monogamy was challenging, consider some of these possible polyamorous arrangements:

Dyad—A sexual love relationship consisting of two primary partners.

Multi-mate relationship—Relationships involving three or more people in which all partners are primary.

Open relationship—Both partners agree to allow each other to have other sexual partners.

Polyfidelity—A closed-group marriage (or marriage-like relationship), in which all adult members are considered primary to each other.

Primary relationship—A committed, long-term, live-in relationship.

Secondary relationship—An ongoing relationship in which the partners usually do not live together and do not consider their relationship a first priority.

Tertiary relationship—A friendly but casual relationship of an occasional or temporary nature.

Triad or quad—Three- or four-way relationships, respectively, in which all participants are considered to be in primary relationships with each other.

Vee—When one person has a relationship with two others who are not involved with each other.

If male homosexuals are called "gay," then female homosexuals should be called "ecstatic."

—Shelly Roberts,
columnist and author

Chapter Eleven

QUEERIES

Gaydar Love

It is generally considered in poor taste to run up to someone whose sexual orientation is in question and ask, "So, are you queer or what?" How do you politely find out if someone is gay? Honestly, it's really none of your business. If said person is someone you are interested in sleeping with, however, a quick tuning of your "gaydar" should help you out. What is that, you ask? Gaydar is not so easy to explain. As a gay male friend of mine tells me, it's instinct. "I just know," he tells me. "Though I have to admit, half the time, my gaydar doesn't work."

Does she own more than one Melissa Etheridge album, wear Birkenstocks or own any of the Moosewood vegetarian cookbook series? I joke, of course, because, as far as I know, there is no lesbian litmus test. And while stereotypes of lesbians abound, they come in many different models, especially these days, as gender and sexual identity become more fluid. You could always try asking her out; if she's not gay, she'll probably turn you down. Of course, she might turn you down even is she is a lesbian, and you still won't know. But now it doesn't matter.

What the Canuck!

1969: Justice Minister Pierre Trudeau's proposed amendments to the Criminal Code, which, among other things, relax the laws against homosexuality, are passed. Discussing the amendments two years earlier, Trudeau says, "There's no place for the state in the bedrooms of the nation."

December 16, 1977: Quebec includes sexual orientation in its Human Rights Code, making it the first province in Canada to pass a gay civil rights law. The law makes it illegal to discriminate against gays in housing, public accommodation and employment. By 2001 all provinces and territories take this step, excluding Alberta, Prince Edward Island and the Northwest Territories.

February 5, 1981: More than 300 men are arrested following police raids at four gay bathhouses in Toronto. The next night, about 3,000 people march in downtown Toronto to protest the arrests.

November 1992: The federal court lifts the country's ban on homosexuals in the military, allowing gays and lesbians to serve in the armed forces.

May 1995: An Ontario Provincial Court judge rules that four lesbians have the right to adopt their partners' children. Ontario becomes the first province to make it legal for same-sex couples to adopt. British Columbia, Alberta and Nova Scotia follow suit.

June 1996: The federal government passes Bill C-33, which adds "sexual orientation" to the *Canadian Human Rights Act*.

May 2002: Marc Hall, a 17-year-old from Oshawa, Ontario, is forbidden by the Durham Catholic School Board to attend his high-school prom with his 21-year-old boyfriend on the grounds that the Catholic Church could not condone a homosexual lifestyle. Ontario Superior Court justice Robert McKinnon rules that Hall has the right to take his boyfriend to the prom.

January 1, 2003: The proud parents of Yukon Territory's first New Year's baby of 2003 are two moms! Their baby girl was born around four a.m. on New Year's Day at Whitehorse General Hospital.

June 10, 2003: The Ontario Court of Appeal upholds a lower court ruling to allow same-sex marriages. Hours after the ruling, Michael Leshner and Michael Stark are married in a ceremony in Toronto.

June 17, 2003: Prime Minister Jean Chrétien announces legislation to make same-sex marriages legal, while at the same time permitting churches and other religious groups to "sanctify marriage as they see it." The case on same-sex marriage isn't expected to be heard by the Supreme Court until early 2004. (Source: CBC)

Gay wonder

I once had a rather embarrassing incident at a bar at four in the morning when I decided to proclaim my love for a guy I'd known for a while. He looked at me, rather shocked, and said, "You do know I'm gay, right, Jose?" Well, sometimes, no, we don't. How do you handle it when the man of your dreams turns out to be playing for the other team? Gracefully, of course. Most guys, even gay guys, will be flattered you thought them sex-worthy. Put away your fantasies that

Quickie

The Mayans of Central America preferred boys to engage in homosexuality until they were able to marry. Parents would provide their son with a slave companion to satisfy his sexual needs rather than run the risk of finding an unmarried girl for the purpose. (Source: Sarah Dening, *The Mythology of Sex*)

you'll be the one to make him switch teams and simply laugh it off. His ego will be stroked, and yours will remain intact. And, if you're lucky, you may have just gained yourself a new "girlfriend."

But what if you start swapping fashion advice with some hottie at the bar, assuming he's gay, only to find out he isn't when you suggest setting him up with your gay male friend? Some straight boys get all bent out of shape when you think they're gay, but I figure the kind of straight boys I'm interested in getting to know should be cool about it. What's the big deal, after all? When people tell me they think I'm a lesbian, I simply thank them and move on. Hopefully, he'll be able to laugh about it too, and it'll be one of those things you fondly look back on when you live happily ever after. Or at least over dinner.

Queer talk

Gay terminology changes with the times. While "fag" and "queer" were once considered put-downs, gays have taken the sting out by "reclaiming" these terms as their own. Here are a few currently relevant terms that might come in handy at your next gay cocktail party:

Gay guide

Barebacking—Engaging in sex without a condom.

Bathhouse—Place where gay men go for anonymous sex. Also known as a sauna.

Bear—A hairy and often hefty gay man.

Daddy or Sugar daddy—An older gay man who has sex with and/or provides for a younger gay man.

Glory hole—Hole in a bathroom stall or wall cut at a strategic level that allows a man to insert his penis and have it serviced orally or manually from the other side.

Size queen—A gay man who prefers large penises.

Tearoom queen—A gay man who likes to have sex in public washrooms.

Lesbian lingo

Androdyke—Short for androgynous dyke. A lesbian who is neither butch nor femme.

Baby butch—A masculine lesbian in her teens or early twenties.

Baby dyke—A young lesbian or one who has just come out; sometimes refers to a soft or smallish butch.

Bull dyke—A masculine lesbian who is also large and strong. Also known as a diesel dyke.

Butch—A lesbian who enacts a traditionally masculine social role.

Drag king—A female (often lesbian) performer who impersonates men, usually within the context of a drag show.

Dykes on bikes—Motorcycle dykes and their girlfriends.

Femme—A lesbian who enacts a more traditionally feminine social role.

Lipstick lesbian—An affectionately satiric term for a feminine lesbian who conforms to heterosexual gender expectations of the way women should look, dress and act.

LUG—Acronym for "lesbian until graduation." Derogative term for a woman who experimented with lesbian relationships in university or college but stopped when she graduated.

Stone butch—A lesbian top who will not allow partners to "service" her in return.

Identifying yourself

Drag queen—A man who dresses in extravagant women's clothing for show and enjoyment. Not all drag queens are transsexuals, transvestites or gay.

FTM—A female-to-male transsexual.

Gender identity—The gender, male or female, you most feel like emotionally and psychologically, regardless of whether you were born biologically male or female.

LGBT—Acronym standing for lesbian, gay, bisexual and transgender.

MTF—A male-to-female transsexual.

Post-op transsexual—A transsexual who has undergone the full surgical procedure (including having the genitals transformed from male to female or vice versa) to change his or her sex.

Pre-op transsexual—Someone who lives as his or her preferred sex but has not yet had, or can't afford, the surgical operations to change his or her sex.

Queer—Homosexual. Originally meaning "odd," the term has been appropriated by the gay community and used as an umbrella term for all those who do not identify as straight.

Sexual orientation—The sex(es) you are attracted to.

Tranny—A slang term for a transsexual or transgender person.

Transgender—A blanket term, independent of sexual orientation, often used to describe those who do not conform to the social roles that those of their biological sex are supposed to play.

Transsexual—Someone who feels that her biological sex does not match her psychological gender. A transsexual usually lives as her preferred gender, and will have operations to change some of the physical aspects of her sex. Transsexuals can be straight, gay or bi.

Transvestite—Someone who wears the clothes of the other sex for fun or for sexual reasons; transvestites do not want to be the other sex. They are usually straight men. A less clinical term used by many transvestites is "cross-dresser," or "CD."

Playing for Both Teams

Revealing to someone that you're bisexual can be tricky. If you're a lesbian sleeping with another lesbian, one presumes the woman you're sleeping with is pretty much okay with homosexuality. If, however, you're bisexual and sleeping with a guy, should you tell him before you sleep with him that you like girls too? I believe no one needs to know your sexual history until he gets to know you better. If you're with someone long enough, presumably he will get to know you and accept you for who you are. If it does come up that you've been with same-sex partners, trust that your partner will be able to handle it. If he can't, it's his loss, really.

That said, I wouldn't toss someone out of bed if he was a little taken aback by the info. Even the most open-minded person can still be challenged by same-sex relationships when they hit close to home. While it is more accepted (even titillating sometimes) to find out a woman has been with other women, the fantasy might be easer to take than the reality. He might also worry that your bisexuality doubles the pool of people you could cheat on him with. Give him time to get used to the idea.

Same goes for a woman who finds out the guy she's sleeping with likes boys. This can be tough for some women to wrap their minds around. As a society, we're still more comfortable seeing women be affectionate with each other than men. It's less of a leap. Most straight men are awkward even hugging each other. How often do you see two young, straight teenage boys walking down the street holding hands (as I often see young teenage girls do)?

Keep an open mind and, if you really can't handle it, don't make him feel like a freak. Take responsibility and simply tell him that it's your problem, but you're just not comfortable. At least you're being honest.

Bi choice

I often get letters from people who are bisexual wondering how to handle their desires for the opposite sex while in a relationship with someone of the same sex, or vice versa. To me the answer seems simple. We all have desires outside our relationships, and we all have to make choices about whether to act upon them. Sure, as a bisexual, you've got double the temptation, but being bisexual doesn't mean you absolutely must sleep with both men and women. It just means you are attracted to both. If you're in a relationship, you still have the same obligation to be faithful. As a bisexual friend once told me, "Being bisexual does not give you license to be an asshole." Bisexuals have a hard enough time battling the stereotype that they're fence-sitters who want it all. Best not to perpetuate it. If you're bisexual and in a relationship but want to continue to sleep with both men and women, you have three choices:

- Live with your feelings but choose not to act on them for the sake of your relationship, just like the rest of us poor monogamous slobs have to do.
- Work out an open relationship so that you and your partner (fair's fair!) get a little action on the side.
- Stay single and sleep with whomever you want.

Bar Code

As a straight woman, I enjoy going to lesbian bars, partly because the music is often better, but also because it can be a nice break from the "meet" market. But there is certain etiquette that should be honoured. Much like travelling to a foreign country, it is important to be aware of cultural differences so you can avoid social blunders and fully enjoy what the culture has to offer.

Consider these rules of conduct:

- Don't bring a guy unless he's gay. No, it's not that lesbians hate men. It's just that one of the reasons lesbian bars exist is to create an all-woman space free of any of the crap women have to deal with when men are around. Go with another woman or go alone.
- Don't try to pass. If you're not a lesbian, or if you don't know whether you are, don't tell women you are. You can't just let yourself into the club without a membership (though most lesbians can smell a straight woman a mile away—it's like gaydar in reverse).
- Be upfront about your status. If a woman hits on you, it's only fair that she know what's she's getting into before she invests any time or emotion. Not all lesbians are willing to indulge a straight girl's fantasy or experimentation (though some certainly are). Give her the choice.
- If you are uncomfortable with women hitting on you, there is no need to stand on the bar and announce your heterosexual status. Just leave.
- Be a good guest. Just as when you are in someone else's home, respect the house rules and always say please and thank you.

Mature Choices

You're married with grown children, and suddenly you find yourself considering an affair, not with a man but with a woman. You're not the only one. It seems there is a growing trend of women who don't necessarily want to leave the life they have established with their husband but, with the children out of the nest, find themselves seeking the company of women, and not just for bridge.

I know an older woman who didn't have sex with her husband for years and left him for a woman simply because, as a feminist back in the fifties, she couldn't find any men who could relate to her. A sudden interest in women may just be intrigue—I won't disagree that the older women get, the more interesting they get—but there are also plenty of women who realize later in life that they are lesbians who married and had children simply because coming out as a lesbian was not acceptable when they were younger. After years of marriage, coming out could mean busting up a family, divorce and having to start a whole new life. Compared to all that, an affair seems like a much simpler option.

But an affair is an affair, and whether with a man or a woman, affairs almost always mess up marriages. So unless you and your husband both agree on an arrangement where you allow each other to see people outside the marriage, you must be prepared for the potential consequences.

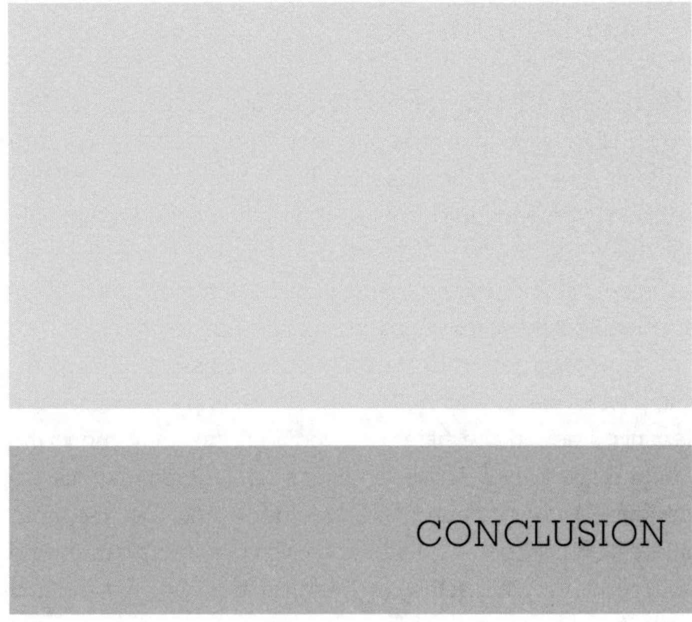

CONCLUSION

A Final Impression

While sexual mores, beliefs, and practices may change through the years, basic conscientiousness, civility and grace are traits that never go out of style.

Just like a bad house guest who doesn't think to leave behind a bottle of wine or at least some flowers to acknowledge the hospitality of their host, even the sexiest-looking woman lessens her chance of a return invite if she displays bad bedside manners. (And if you're not hoping for a return visit, it's preferable to leave a good impression anyway.)

I hope this book has convinced you that sexual etiquette is not about adhering to social expectations or pressures, but conducting a sexual life that is mutually respectful, empowering and joyful.

While I have tried to cover as many bases as possible, there are undoubtedly sexual situations for which the proper decorum is not outlined in this book. If you have any more sexual etiquette questions, please send them along to me at jvogels@mymessybedroom.com.

BIBLIOGRAPHY

Books and Articles

Dening, Sarah. *The Mythology of Sex: An Illustrated Exploration of Sexual Customs and Practices from Ancient Times to the Present*. Sydney: Random House Australia, 1996.

Gilbert, Harriett, and Christine Roche. *A Women's History of Sex*. Kitchener, ON: Pandora Press, 1987.

Gudgeon, Chris. *The Naked Truth: The Untold Story of Sex in Canada*. Vancouver: Greystone Books, 2003.

Kellogg, John Harvey. *Plain Facts for Old and Young: Natural History and Hygiene of Organic Life*. F. Segner, 1888.

Lady Green. *The Compleat Spanker*. Oakland: Greenery Press, 1998.